"I Can't Believe I'm Sitting Next to a Republican"

"I Can't Believe I'm Sitting Next to a Republican"

A Survival Guide for Conservatives

Marooned Among the Angry, Smug,

and Terminally Self-Righteous

BY

HARRY STEIN

ENCOUNTER BOOKS
NEW YORK · LONDON

First edition published in 2009 by Encounter Books,
an activity of Encounter for Culture and Education, Inc.,
a nonprofit, tax exempt corporation.
Encounter Books website address: www.encounterbooks.com

Manufactured in the United States and printed on
acid-free paper. The paper used in this publication meets
the minimum requirements of ANSI/NISO Z39.48_1992
(R 1997) (Permanence of Paper).

FIRST EDITION

LIBRARY OF CONGRESS CATALOGING IN PUBLICATION DATA

Stein, Harry, 1948–
"I can't believe I'm sitting next to a Republican" : a survival guide for con-
servatives marooned among the angry, smug, and terminally self-righteous
/ by Harry Stein.
p. cm.
Includes bibliographical references and index.
ISBN-13: 978-1-59403-253-0 (hardcover : alk. paper)
ISBN-10: 1-59403-253-x (hardcover : alk. paper)
1. Conservatism—United States. 2. United States—Politics and
government—2001– 3. Stein, Harry, 1948– 4. Stein, Harry, 1948—
Political and social views. 5. Authors, American—20th century—
Biography. 6. Journalists—United States—Biography. I. Title.
JC573.2.U6S74 2009
320.520973—dc22
2008048677

10 9 8 7 6 5 4 3 2 1

Contents

Denotes the capacity to thrive, values and beliefs unsullied, in environments where the most repellant liberal attitudes and social customs hold sway.

Awarded to those individuals who stand up for conservative principles in the face of withering scorn and contempt, and at significant risk of professional opprobrium. Notable recent winners include actress Patricia Heaton, Harvard professor Harvey Mansfield, CNBC's Rick Santelli, and master playwright David Mamet, for his gift of the ultimate word on NPR. (See p.144.)

Notes from the Belly of the Beast

THE PHONE MESSAGES and emails from fellow conservatives started coming early on election night 2008 and continued well into the next day. Some were anguished, some merely fatalistic. But even most of these featured at least a dollop of gallows humor.

"Just thought I'd check in before I went out back and slashed my wrists," went the message on my answering machine from my friend Ron, who'd recently moved from New York to North Carolina seeking also a change of political climate. "What a bloodbath, huh? Our country and the world are about to be cast into ruin. Talk to you soon."

My friend David couldn't help venting about the disgracefully in-the-tank-for-Obama media. "They dealt with every story potentially damaging to Obama like it was Rasputin. They didn't just bury it – they shot, poisoned and drowned it!"

Then there was my friend Cary, who, as the dimensions of the disaster became apparent late on election night, announced he might have to skip work.

"For how long?" I asked.

"I'm thinking a year."

Who could blame him? Obama may be our worst nightmare, front man for every species of noxious, left-wing activism going, but at least he makes open-minded noises. In Manhattan offices like my friend's his acolytes don't even bother pretending to civility.

Elisabeth Hasselbeck, the token conservative on "The View," was among those who made the mistake of going to work the morning after. "I fought hard on the other side, but today is a victory for this country," she graciously allowed on the air. "I haven't felt this good throughout this entire election process."

"So what you are saying is I was right all along?" shot back her colleague Joy Behar.

My friend John Leo forwarded the missive from one Blue State blogger summing up what Behar surely wishes she could have said out loud: "Aaaaaaaaaaaahahahaahaaaaaa!! He's dead, it's dead, the Republican beast is fucking deaaaaaaaaad!! Eight years of that rampaging Republican fucking elephant beast finally brought to its knees! Yes, you're dead, you fucker, you fuck, you fuck, you're Dead! Dead! Dead! "

Of course, there are those who'll argue that the authors of such remarks are the hothead fringe of the vast, untidy American left – modern liberalism's equivalent of the leather-lunged townsfolk in old Westerns shouting, "What're we waitin' for, let's string 'im up!" Most liberals, they'll say, are far more level-headed than that.

And they're absolutely right. Ordinary liberals are the ones in the mob who, on hearing the hotheads' bloodthirsty cries, mumble for a second or two and then go along with the plan.

This book is about those who are not part of the mob at all, the conservatives living and working among such folk – and, more than occasionally, the ones getting lynched. They are the good guys in this story. Think of them as Gary Cooper in *High Noon*, strong, independent, ready to risk their lives (okay, sometimes their careers, and always a nasty comment) on principle.

Indeed, their very day-to-day experience reveals how utterly deformed is the current version of liberalism. It presents stark evidence of the extent to which a philosophy predicated on freedom of thought and openness to varied perspectives has become a wellspring of intolerance and rancor.

Here, for instance, is just a tiny, *tiny* sample, courtesy of the

Huffington Post, of how liberal *New York Times* readers reacted to the news, in the closing days of 2007, that in a touching bid to recapture a bit of its vanished credibility as a somewhat even-handed journal, the paper would be running a weekly column by the conservative eminence William Kristol on its op-ed page.

- Worthless suck-up Kristol should be cleaning toilets in public restrooms for his GOP "friends."
- I will never, ever buy another issue of the newspaper, I will never again be a subscriber to your newspaper, and I will do my level best to avoid any purchases from any *New York Times* advertiser.
- William "the Bloody" Kristol is a beady-eyed warmonger. . .
- If *The New York Times* is going to hire a liar and a racist like Bill Kristol, then they might as well hire Rush Limbaugh, Sean Hannity, Ann Coulter, Michael Savage, Bill O'Reilly, and Ari Fleischer.
- Kristol is an arrogant, warmongering prick. I can't stand the sight of him.
- Just what *The New York Times* needs, another stenographer for the right-wing slime machine.
- Listening to Kristol, that warmongering crater-face, is worse than listening to Bush, Cheney, and Richard Perle all rolled up in one. . . . I hate that decision and I will do everything I can to discredit this decision until they finally flush him down the toilet like the turd he is.

Not to worry. Exactly a year later, when Kristol's contract was up, the *Times* unceremoniously dumped him.

To be sure, the conservatives I'll deal with herein are difficult to pigeonhole. They – okay, we – are a diverse lot. Personally, though an out and proud libertarian-conservative, I actually remain a registered Democrat; partly because of inertia, *mainly* because the GOP is so pathetically off-base or weak-kneed on many of the issues I care about, from government spending to affirmative action. Besides, as a New Yorker, I want my say on primary day. (That's when my wife and I work our own private Operation Chaos – voting for Al Sharpton whenever his name appears on the ballot and otherwise doing our modest bit to mess with the party's head).

While by definition most every conservative getting by in the alien environment of Blue State America is blessed with independent judgment and a fair amount of backbone, a working sense of humor doesn't hurt, either. How else to deal with the stuff that at any time can put a crimp in an otherwise fine day – the angry old lady with the anti-war sign affixed to her walker, the PETA zealots from the nearby campus, or the random leftist idiot at a dinner party, waxing self-righteous and quoting George Soros?

One friend of mine recalls being interrupted by an infuriated fellow shopper on Broadway half a block from Zabar's. She'd overheard him speaking approvingly about the War on Terror to a friend. "I can't believe I'm hearing this – and on the Upper West Side!" Then, he recalls, laughing at the memory, "she fled in terror, as if looking for a commissar to report us to."

The fact is, in key ways, those of us living and working among such people often know them better than they know themselves. Unable as we are to avoid the media they take as gospel – NPR, the networks, *The New York Times* or its local equivalent – we're on intimate terms with their most passionately held beliefs and convictions. We know who they admire and who they despise; we know in advance how they'll react to every controversy, every utterance by a public figure; we anticipate, politically and public policy-wise, their sighs, their frowns, their ups, their downs.

Existing as we do in both worlds – leading, as it were, double lives – those of us on the right get to experience the remarkable liberal mindset on a daily basis, up close and personal. Among the many things of which we are frequently reminded is how astonishingly little they know about us. What they think they know, they've picked up by innuendo or, very nearly the same thing, the commentary in their preferred media. It can be boiled down to this: Conservatives are greedy, hard-hearted, evil bastards, and are, by definition, wrong about absolutely everything. More than a few liberals would, if they could, make us wear warning bells like medieval lepers, and force us to shout, on every approach, "Unclean! Unclean!" (Maybe they will, after Obama gets to appoint a Supreme Court justice or two!)

But what might be most startling about the liberals is their capacity for self-delusion. Not long ago, Dennis Prager produced a splendid column called "When I Was a Boy, America Was a Better Place." Basically, it was a catalogue of the disasters liberalism has visited upon American culture in recent decades.

· Restrictions on free (and honest) speech in the name of sensitivity.

· The remaking of American history into therapy for minorities and women.

· A general decline in civility.

· The absence of fathers from countless homes.

· The stigmatization of men as potential predators.

· The corruption of childhood through an aggressively sexualized culture.

What's funny, if that's the word, is that even those comparatively reasonable liberals who decry these and other cultural changes cited by Prager seem to have no idea that any of them stem from liberalism. As one such guy I know put it, apparently oblivious to the contradiction, liberalism "stands for progress; conservatism stands for turning back the clock to the bad old days."

In fact, what we conservatives stand for is a commitment

to enduring verities and immutable standards, which is quite a different thing. Meanwhile, for liberals, the very meaning of that magic word "progress" is subject to constant and even violent revision.

As a reformed lib myself, I vividly recall how, during the debate on the Equal Rights Amendment in the early Seventies, my friends and I used to sneer at the ERA opponents' claims that its passage would lead one day to co-ed bathrooms on college campuses and women in combat. We labeled these arguments absurd right-wing canards designed to scare the hell out of credulous Middle Americans. A couple of decades later, countless millions of liberals themselves were dismissing the notion of gay marriage as an outright absurdity. Today, in liberal land, to so much as question the desirability of any of these things is to cast suspicion upon oneself as a closet reactionary.

I swear, to try and find any logic in it is to make one's head spin.

Of course, that's precisely the point. When you're talking liberalism, you may be talking many things – self-righteousness, good intentions as an end in themselves, obliviousness to consequences – but logic is not one of them. Liberals feel what they feel, when they feel it, and what they feel at any given moment is what they *know*.

This is why anyone who believes that a liberal can be straightened out if only reality is explained to him, simply and clearly, is doomed to fail. I made that mistake myself some years back, at book length. That volume was entitled *How I Accidentally Joined the Vast Right-Wing Conspiracy (and Found Inner Peace)*, and I truly expected that (a) most of its readers would be liberals curious to know why one of their own would desert the tribe and (b) it might engender some interesting conversation across ideological lines.

The reader is free to imagine me smashing my forehead and exclaiming "D'oh!"

Truly, I've never been so wrong about anything in my life. I literally cannot say with complete certainty that a single liberal even read it. And I include family and friends, none of whom seems to have gotten past the most cursory skim. One old friend, in a moment of unembarrassed candor, told me he read the title and "was sickened." Another, a guy on my over-forty softball team, *claimed* to have read it, sneeringly referring to it as *How I Lost All My Ethics and Became a Fascist*, but when closely questioned didn't seem to know anything that was in it.

It is a mistake I won't make again. This book is not only about, but also expressly *for*, those who already know exactly what I'm talking about – those for whom a red flag goes up every time they see the words "diversity," "multicultural," or "non-judgmental."

As it happens, there are lots and lots and lots of us out there, a good many more, in fact, than we sometimes realize, in our apparent isolation. Even the 2008 election results, gruesome as they were, make that abundantly clear. Let's put it this way: In Cambridge, Massachusetts, where a lunatic like Noam Chomsky is considered mainstream, the McCain–Palin ticket got 4,664 votes; in San Francisco, which lays out the welcome mat for the drug-addled homeless like other cities do for free-spending conventioneers, an intrepid Republican named Dana Walsh racked up 16,149 versus Nancy Pelosi (and never mind that *Cindy Sheehan* outpolled Walsh nearly 2–1); in Chicago, Congressman Jesse Jackson Jr.'s intrepid Republican opponent drew 29,050 voters, not a single one residing in a cemetery; and, yes, even in Manhattan's Upper West Side, ground zero for elitist know-it-alls, media narcissists, airheads in the arts and America-hating academics, the Republican challenger to formerly rotund liberal icon Jerry Nadler polled 35,822.

As a matter of fact, this book's working title was *Red Manhattan*, the reference of course being to Red State-types marooned on that magnificent, accursed island. But I soon saw that the title provoked confusion. Some took it to refer to Communists of old, of which there were plenty in Manhattan, and others objected on geographical grounds, since I was dealing not just with beleaguered conservatives in New York, but anywhere self-satisfied liberal ignorance holds sway.

Among the alternatives I considered were *In Darkest Blue America*, *Among the Savages in Darkest Blue America*, and *Behind Enemy Lines*, and each was obviously wanting. But, as we know, in their perverse way, liberals never fail to come through. I was still struggling with the title problem when, one evening, my wife and I attended a dinner party. It was primary season, early on in Obama mania, and when, inevitably, the discussion turned to the glories of The Messiah, I felt compelled to sound a mild cautionary note about his lack of experience. At this, the guy beside me, who'd known me all of fifteen minutes, drew back his chair, cast me a savage look, and roared, inaccurately, "I can't believe I'm sitting next to a Republican!"

This is the sort of thing known, in the liberal academy, (or would be, were I of the appropriate gender and pigmentation), as a "hate speech," and who's to say that it won't soon become a federal crime? But we conservatives know how to take it – and far worse – in stride.

Indeed, during the presidential campaign, infuriated liberals cast even the mildest criticism of Obama as racist, and in the bluest of Blue State locales, to flout the local belief system involved genuine courage. It's anyone's guess how many thousands of conservative cars got keyed – ours, for one, $1700 dollars worth. In Seattle, a leftist weekly, *The Stranger*, actually pointed vandals in the right direction, by printing the addresses and photos of local houses with McCain yard signs.

Then again, no auto-related expression of liberal rage compares with the experience of a certain Gareth Groves – and that wasn't even around election time. One morning a couple of years back, Groves, 38, emerged from his home in the tony Northwest section of Washington, D.C., to find that someone had taken a baseball bat to the windows and body of his month-old $38,000

Hummer, and a machete to the interior, and then, almost redundantly, etched on the side the words "FOR THE ENVIRON."

According to the *Washington Post*, his neighbors reacted to this as liberals will. While some professed misgivings about the violence involved, others pretty much thought he'd gotten what he deserved. Reporting the story in a tone best described as bemused, the *Post* reporter pointed out that, after all, Mr. Groves's was an extremely "socially conscious" and "environmentally friendly neighborhood," one rich in Priuses and other hybrids, and since acquiring his gas-guzzling behemoth he'd often been subjected to angry stares and hostile comments. Indeed, one neighbor, freely identifying herself by name, was moved to declare acidly that "he's very proud of himself that he has such a macho vehicle. It belongs in a war zone. Send it to Iraq."

Some might think of Gareth Groves as a poor schnook living in the wrong place at the wrong time, or as a naïve fool for believing he could so heedlessly rile up the local enviro-vigilantes without paying the price. Lots of us know better. We see him as the exemplar of personal courage that he is, a free-market, free-thinking individualist amidst the herd of independent minds: Gary Cooper in *High Noon*, contentedly ensconced in a seven-foot, 122.8 wheelbased steel and chrome horse.

My Home Town
(*and Keith Olbermann's*)

WHERE EVEN THE VILLAGE IDIOT
READS *THE NEW YORK TIMES*

THE TOWN WHERE we live, the New York suburb of Hastings-on-Hudson, is as attractive to the eye as its name suggests – a leafy hamlet, with spectacular river views and a little downtown area largely unchanged since the Fifties. When my wife and I, looking for a place to raise our two young children, came upon it almost twenty-five years ago, we couldn't believe our good luck. A mere half hour from the city, it had the neighborly charm of the classic small town. Back then, it seemed every fifth car bore the same bumper sticker; although, in our urban cynicism, we privately smiled at the hickish boosterism, we fully endorsed the sentiment: "Hastings is a neat place to live."

In most ways, it still is. There's fireworks by the river every Fourth of July; the Farmers Market all year round; the sounds of kids sledding in Hillside Park on snow days; the crack of aluminum on Clincher softballs summer Sundays (guys like me, deluding ourselves we can still play, have a fiercely competitive over-40 league); there's the fabulous library and an ever-enterprising local historical society. Crime is low and civic morale high.

Then there are the people. As always, it's almost impossible to stop in at the Center Restaurant for a ham and cheese on rye and not run into two or three or four people you know. Wandering down the aisles of the A&P, you're apt at any moment to find yourself catching up with someone about the kids, or bemoaning the stupidity of the Mets front office, or speculating about the new shop going in where The Office Ink used to be. How does the song go? "I love those dear hearts and gentle people, who live in my home town"?

But a word of warning: Don't get onto politics. If you do, things between you and the dear heart and gentle person before you are likely to change.

To say Hastings is liberal is like saying Saudi Arabia is Muslim. While there are relatively few outright lunatics, there are enough lunatic fellow travelers that fitting in means accepting a lot of lunatic norms. In this and other ways, we are a suburban version of Manhattan's Upper West Side – the very area from which many of my neighbors decamped in settling here. (Okay, so did we.) The place is chock full of mainstream media types, therapists, executives of do-gooding foundations, environmental lawyers, and, last but hardly least, the creative set – writers, actors, photographers, directors, set designers, and so on. The town takes great pride in these creative types, in many cases justifiably, but it must be said that they've brought with them the same love of intellectual diversity for which the Upper West Side is so renowned. To sum up: The hyperventilating leftist madman Keith Olbermann grew up in Hastings, and, boy, would he ever fit in these days!

To the casual observer, this might not be immediately apparent. The vast majority of my neighbors are too busy living their lives to waste much time on politics. They vote Democratic for the same reason they watch their diet and floss their teeth – it's what smart, responsible, healthy, forward-thinking people do.

That is to say that when, at a neighborhood gathering, one of these people suddenly learns that your views deviate from everyone else's on the war, affirmative action, big government, feminism, Jimmy Carter, the environment, multiculturalism, sex education, the reliability of *The New York Times*, the scariness of evangelicals, or (hell, fill in the blank), his or her face will register stunned surprise and deep confusion. You can almost see the wheels turning within and hear the electronic drone: *Does not compute.* After all, in most ways you *seem* reasonable; your knuckles don't drag the ground. Yet the things coming out of your mouth sound so wrong – almost *conservative.* Which, as everyone knows (without actually knowing anything about it), is just another way of saying warmongering, racist, homophobic, not to mention terminally uptight and ready to wipe out every last polar bear for the sake of Big Oil.

But such a person will not hate you.

In fact, few such encounters end badly. After all, you, the conservative, are also a *neighbor*, and you otherwise get along fine. So the confused liberal will simply change the subject or, at worst, after an awkward pause, excuse himself to get something to drink. What will *not* happen is an actual exchange of ideas, since, by definition, your ideas (even if they were to be accorded that lofty status), are bad and dangerous.

But, then, there's another kind of liberal you're sure to run into, the fierce and angry lefty partisan, fairly dripping with contempt for everything you are and represent. These are far less numerous – over my more than two decades in Hastings, I've had no more than a dozen encounters with such people. Yet each encounter has been, in its own special way, memorably unpleasant.

I had a couple of such incidents during the 2008 presidential campaign, when Palin Derangement Syndrome took an especially brutal toll on local women. Then there was the one that occurred in the supermarket, around the time the controversy about waterboarding was at its height. I was on the checkout line, behind a huge bearded guy I knew slightly, because his son had once played on a baseball team I coached. So I nodded.

I could see him hesitate. Suddenly, he spat out: "You people disgust me!"

"Excuse me?" I asked, startled.

"You Bush lovers!" he said, his neck muscles starting to work and his face going crimson. "All that bullshit you put the country through over a little lie about sex, but you have no problem at all with torture!"

Of course, the guy had no idea what I thought about Bush (which happened to be not much), or torture, or anything else, and his pegging me as an Administration bitter-ender could not have been more off-base. But he knew I'd written a conservative book, so what more did he need?

There are assorted theories as to how to deal with such frothing maniacs, but given the fact that this is Hastings – there was zero chance that the guy was armed, and, for all his menace, he probably considered himself a pacifist – I felt comfortable showing him all the respect he deserved. "Hey, c'mon," I said, shooting him the best mocking smile I could muster, "how else you gonna get the information out of those bastards?"

"You're disgusting," he sputtered, swiping up his shopping bag and stomping away. "You sicken me!"

"Know what?" I called after him. "You're a *really* angry guy."

He wheeled around. "There's plenty to be angry about!"

Again, there is only a relative handful of people like this in our community. But here's the problem: Like perpetually aggrieved leftists everywhere, they tend to be activists, and in a place like Hastings they are deferred to by other, lesser liberals for their passion and what is taken to be their command of issues. They play an outsized role in setting the tone for the place; they are ubiquitous in their angry letters to the editor in the local paper, their meetings against the war or global warming, and their appearances en masse at governmental meetings to push their agendas.

Why does this matter? They are self-anointed "good people," and in various and often unexpected ways, the rest of us are obliged to live in their smug and narrow world. A tiny example. A couple of years back, the village decided to put up little placards marking local spots of historic interest – the site where Peter

Post's Revolutionary-era tavern once stood, for example, or the fact that the Village Hall was designed by the same firm that did the Empire State Building. Dubbed the "Museum of the Streets," it was a lovely idea – except that when the signs appeared, they were in English *and Spanish*, never mind that our local Spanish-speaking population is extremely close to zero.

Of course, for local liberals, the bilingual signs served a political and (redundantly, since so often the two are indistinguishable) moral purpose. They were a reminder, in the unlikely event that anyone needed one, of where we, as big-hearted progressives, stand on the issue of "so-called illegal aliens."

Oh yeah, and when the Hastings Little League was adding a minor league division, you think the new teams got named after big league clubs, the way they do it in other places? Are you kidding? Where's the nobility in *that*? Stop by Uniontown Field or Zinnser Park on a lovely late spring afternoon and you'll find kids in this overwhelmingly white, upper-middle-class town with "Barons," "Grays," and "Monarchs" across their little chests – teams from the old Negro Leagues.

If one allows it to be, this kind of stuff can be a constant, low-level irritant, an ideological mosquito impossible to kill. The local weekly doesn't help. For instance, the lead story on the front page of a recent issue, headlined "Concert Aims to Help Heal the Planet," brims with admiration for a twenty-two-year-old local singer/songwriter who "brought together local musicians, speakers, entertainers, and others" for a planet-healing concert and "then went door to door to local businesses soliciting donations for the concert." Fine. Idealism in the young is indeed to be applauded. Yet it is more than a little off-putting that no one on the paper's editorial staff would ever consider the possibility that, in fact, the very premises behind the global warming hysteria are open to debate. And one can only guess at the paper's reaction – let alone that of Riverspa, Eileen Fisher, Green Babies, Black Cat Café, Sunnyside Florist, and Ivkosic Painting Corp., among other local donor businesses – if some idealistic twenty-two-year-old was going around soliciting dough on behalf of, say, a campaign against racial preferences.

One recent local election, the Republican caucus drew exactly four people, and they decided not even to bother fielding a candidate for either of the two trustee slots that would appear on the ballot. The same night, the Democratic caucus attracted nearly a thousand. Then again, the Dems had some pressing business, since the leadership had decided to get rid of two Democratic incumbent trustees for the sin of being insufficiently anti-development, and to replace them with individuals more inflexible in their dogmatic leftism.

It didn't used to be this way in Hastings. Through most of the twentieth century it was primarily a factory town, with the chemical and Anaconda copper plants down by the river manned by first- and second-generation Slavs, Italians, and Poles. (Don't bother looking for signs in any of *those* languages.)

Yet, for some reason, it also attracted lots of artistic types, at one point being home to both *The Wizard of Oz's* Good Witch Glinda, Billie Burke, and to Frank Morgan, the Wizard himself. Over the years, there were also some notable leftists, including the legendary birth-control crusader (and eugenics enthusiast) Margaret Sanger, and Abel Meeropol, the composer of the anti-lynching classic "Strange Fruit." Meeropol, with his wife, took in and raised the sons of Julius and Ethel Rosenberg after the couple's execution up the river at Sing-Sing. Daniel Ellsberg, the Pentagon Papers leaker, also graced our little town with his presence. So did the Nobel-winning economist William Vickrey – a subscriber during World War II to the monthly *The Conscientious Objector*, a complete set of which I now own, along with an array of other fascinating political material, thanks to a rummage sale at his home after his death.

No problem with any of that. In a town as varied politically as it was ethnically and economically, it was all part, as the diversity mongers like to say, of Hastings's "glorious tapestry." (Hell, back in the early Fifties, the town welcomed the teenage daughter of Hitler confidante Albert Speer, who spent a year here as an exchange student.) Hard to believe now, but when we moved to Hastings, the town had a *Republican* mayor.

Things started to change around the late Eighties. That's when Baby Boom types – i.e., people like us – began flooding into the place from the city. As real estate went through the roof, lots of old-timers cashed out and left. Well, no, not all of them. Many have just kind of receded into the background, so that the gruff old guy with the Russian accent at the hardware store or the woman selling the homemade pierogies in the church sale are just part of the local color, like the Palisades.

In fact, there are probably a lot more conservatives around town than one would think from the local vote totals or the stuff that gets into *The Rivertowns Enterprise*. "I know plenty of people who agree with us," confides one conservative fellow-traveler, a teacher who doubles as a volunteer fireman. "Most of the business owners in town, police officers, firefighters, electricians, plumbers, roofers. All those who have to deal with the realities that most liberals never face. And those people resent the shit out of those who now run the town and the schools, and tell everyone else what they're supposed to think and do."

No question that's true. Some of the very best political conversations I've had in this town over the years have been with guys I was paying to get the toilet flushing and keep the ceiling from falling down. They always seem every bit as delighted to be having these conversations as I am – and, in light of my obvious shortcomings as a homeowner (which is to say, as a man), a lot more surprised.

Then again, given their respect for economic realities, when in other homes, dealing with other toilets and ceilings, most of

7

them tend to keep pretty quiet about it. In Hastings as elsewhere, it is the rare tradesman who blithely mixes business with inflammatory politics. I actually thought I saw such an intrepid soul not long ago on Main Street, where I was stopped at a traffic light. She appeared from one of the stores, hauling some trash out to the curb, a heavy-set, middle-aged bottle blonde wearing, get this, a FREEDOM IS NOT FREE t-shirt.

"You're pretty brave to be wearing that around here!" I called, as the light changed.

"Hey," she called after, "I don't give half a fuck what anyone thinks!"

Not exactly my style, but in these parts right-wingers can't be choosers. I returned to Main Street later that day, hoping to find the woman and get her story, but no one had seen her or seemed to know who she was. It was like trying to hunt down the elusive One-Armed Man in *The Fugitive*, and after a while I began to wonder if she might have been a figment of my desperate conservative imagination.

Every now and then, I discover that some longtime acquaintance has been a secret political soulmate all along. It happened not long ago with a guy I've known casually for years through softball and Little League. We were riding into the city on the train, when he let drop a mildly disparaging remark about Obama – "Not really someone I fully trust with the economy" – then waited to see how I'd take it. "Or with anything else," I replied, and, nodding, he shot me a smile. We were now free to proceed with the entire range of shared assumptions, from the conviction that the President's stimulus plan was most likely to stimulate disaster to the understanding that in *The New York Times*, you're apt to find lies even on the sports page.

In places like our town, this is how we political deviants tend to find one another, via an array of subtle cues that amount to a secret code, the way Communists used to in the days when exposure could get them fired or worse. Of course, these days in Hastings, when it comes to being a Red, *no problema*, as the local signage might put it. A couple of years back, the main speaker at Hastings High's graduation ceremony was actually Rosenberg son and HHS graduate Robbie Meeropol, now grown into a full-fledged activist himself, who to great acclaim denounced the "murder" of his "innocent" parents.

So, one can hardly fault those right-of-center types who keep their views under wraps. "Why get into arguments with people?" as one such guy put it to me, explaining his reluctance to go on the record. "Your kids have to go to school with their kids, and it just leads to no good."

Never is this more true than around presidential election time, when every third car seems to sprout a Democratic bumper sticker, and, on the evidence, none were even printed for the Republicans. Then, again, the prospect of ending up at at a body shop paying a small fortune to undo the work of a vandal for social justice does have something to do with it.

In a place like this, you can be friendly enough with those who hold a worldview diametrically opposed to yours, but those who genuinely share your views are absolute gold, fellow speakers of a forbidden tongue. "You know how I think of myself around here?" laughed my friend Lary Greiner, in one of our frequent heart-to-hearts. "As a one-man conversation stopper. Whenever I offer an opinion in a roomful of Hastings people, the place goes silent. At the beginning, I used to wonder, 'Is my zipper exposed? Is something falling out of my nose? Did I forget to put my teeth in?'"

My friend Tom Smart, like Lary a native Midwesterner cursed with common-sense values, recalls his first encounter with the local political sensibility at a neighborhood party. "It was around the time of Bork's nomination to the Supreme Court," recalls Tom, a big-time Manhattan attorney, "and there were a bunch of women talking very agitatedly about Bork, because of abortion.

So I listened for a while, and then I said 'You know, Robert Bork is the foremost constitutional scholar of his generation. In fact, given his academic credentials and intellectual prowess, some people say he's the most uniquely qualified person ever to be nominated to the Court.'"

He pauses, smiling at his own naïveté. "Was I actually expecting a rational response? It's hard to remember. Anyway, what I got was sputtering rage. It was like I'd said Hitler was a pretty good guy."

Hey, at least it got said to his face. Several Christmases back, my wife returned in high dudgeon from a "charity fair" at a local church. It was one of those events where one could contribute to worthy causes in lieu of gifts, and Priscilla had just made a donation on behalf of African orphans when a guy standing nearby, a teammate on my softball team, offered a characteristic dose of progressive holiday cheer. "Boy," he laughed, presuming that, as a woman, she shared his views, "Harry must really be pissed you're doing this!"

Of course, the following summer, Priscilla's own cover was blown, of all places, on the front page of *The New York Times*. It was in the wake of Hurricane Katrina, when she happened to be waylaid at the local train station by a reporter contributing to a roundup on the "shock" and "shame" and "anger" occasioned by the administration's handling of the tragedy. "Priscilla Turner, 55, of Hastings-on-Hudson, N.Y.," read the story the next day, "said President Bush was being saddled with some unfair blame. 'There is an instinct to be so negative,' Ms. Turner said, 'to wish for the worst, to anticipate the worst, to glory and wallow in the worst.' If Mr. Bush had sent troops to New Orleans too quickly, she said, his detractors would have portrayed him as 'going in with guns blazing.'"

What she'd actually told the reporter was that if Bush had sent in troops and even one looter had been killed, "you guys at *The New York Times* would have savaged him for going in with guns blazing." But never mind. As it was, she was set upon that very afternoon by a neighbor, a woman we'd always thought of as placid and eminently reasonable, who spat out that if it was up to her, the President "would be strung up."

As it happens, my wife is, if anything, even further to the right than I am. She's a onetime Berkeleyite lunatic who now is on intimate terms with dozens of conservative websites. Given to sarcasm and slashing wit, she often comes off in private as a small-town Ann Coulter.

At long last, some of our neighbors were getting a taste of that. At a gathering soon after her appearance in the *Times*, I noticed her in animated conversation with one of our more intemperate liberal neighbors, and edged in closer for a listen. They were talking Native Americans, the liberal taking the conventional view that they were by definition good and noble, and that the appearance of the white man on these shores had been an unmitigated disaster not only for them, but also for the planet and every species of creature on it. "So," my wife shot back, with the snort of derision I know so well, "you'd like to have kept them in the Stone Age, fenced the country off, and turned it into an aboriginal theme park?"

I suspect few of our neighbors any longer make the mistake of thinking she's on their side.

So what's the bottom line? As a conservative in a deep-blue enclave like Hastings, do you sometimes get to feeling pretty isolated? Damn right! Even a little alienated? You bet! I mean, in places like this, you're constantly struck by your distance even from those you regard as friends.

For instance, there's an extremely nice guy named Llyn Clague down the street, with whom I sometimes have lunch. Semi-retired, he not only has a name fit for a poet, but really is one, and quite gifted – or so I'm told by my wife, who actually reads poetry. Anyway, he's not the kind of guy I'd ever thought of as at all political, until one day he handed me a poem entitled "Missing Bush."

It reads, in part:

At cocktail parties, walking the dog, on the train –
An instant bond,
Even with strangers. Again
And again – beyond
Politics – a connection
Between the insistent and the unresigned.
An affection
As much of the heart
As the mind

Like an image reversed through a lens,
Looking through Bush I see humans'
Potential. Scenes of kinder men,
More generous women;
Of reach out to one, or many,
In trouble;
A new Adam, rising out of the rubble.

As I say, I've never been a fan of George W. Bush – in fact, in the fall of 2004, I enjoyed sowing consternation and perplexity in the neighborhood by sporting a bumper sticker for the Libertarian candidate, Michael Badnarik, on our old and eminently keyable Chrysler. Nevertheless, my attitude in both 2000 and 2004 was *far better Bush than the Democratic alternatives* – and, just as much to the point, being a conservative in a town like mine tends to give you a strong, if silent, rooting interest in almost anyone your neighbors loathe.

During the campaign of 2008, the hostility toward me and my

kind ran deeper than ever before. In opposing the Democrats' frighteningly naïve and astonishingly radical candidate, we were seen as opposing not a man, but history itself. More than once, I saw animated conversations on the street come to an abrupt halt at my approach; and it wasn't all that hard to imagine the tenor of some of the things said once I was past.

It's at times like this that you find out who your true friends are. One is my buddy Brian, as gregarious and good hearted a fellow as you'll ever meet. Having noted my rising apprehension as Election Day approached, the night the verdict was in, he left me a bemused but sympathetic message: "I tell you, man, personally I'm pretty excited. But I know how hard it is for you. So I want to let you know I've got your back and you can count on me to protect you from all those nasty liberals."

That is more reassuring than it probably sounds, since Brian once played football for UCLA. But just in case, I have an offer from another friend, a closeted conservative as concerned as I about the collectivist assault on individaul initiative and other looming threats to ideological pluralism. "Listen," he said, when I ran into him a few days after the election, smiling but keeping his voice low, "we've got a big attic. If it comes to it, you guys can hide out up there, like Anne Frank."

The Purple Party

OR, MY WIFE TRIES – AND FAILS –
TO BRIDGE THE GAP

THE NOTION THAT your average liberal is governed by anything even vaguely resembling rationality can only lead to no good.

My wife, bless her, not long ago made the mistake of imagining otherwise and decided to throw what she called a "purple party" – i.e., a mix of red and blue – with three women as invited guests. The chosen liberals were a couple of our otherwise good-hearted and eminently likeable neighbors; the conservative, for want of a suitable local candidate, was a battle-hardened import from Brooklyn. My wife was excited about this, thinking of it as a kind of outreach program. She figured they'd start off talking the usual stuff – kids, jobs, home furnishings – and then, a couple of bottles of Chardonnay in, when everyone was feeling chummy, she'd deftly steer the conversation toward politics and social policy.

Yeah, like *that* was gonna work.

How to say this kindly? The Purple Party was a disaster. Twenty minutes in, there arose some serious unpleasantness about Iraq. Then, a little liquored up, one of the liberal women started telling Bush jokes. Like, for instance, the one about the sweet old lady recently diagnosed with Alzheimer's. "'What's your name?' the doctor asked her, and she answered correctly. 'Where were you born?' Again correct. 'Do you know what day of the week this is?' Right again. Now the doctor asks: 'Which president started the Iraq war?' There's a *looong* pause, as she tries to come up with the answer, and then she remembers: 'The Asshole.'"

A bit before this, my wife, per my request, had snapped on the tape recorder I'd given her. On the tape, you can hear the joke teller and her liberal pal crack up, but from the other two – silence.

Soon they moved on to Hillary Clinton. Since this was New York, and the liberals were part of Hillary's core constituency of white suburban women of a certain age, things went downhill quickly.

"I really can't understand her appeal," said the conservative woman, understating her true opinion, and added that in her view Hillary had only gotten ahead because of her debased husband.

She was interrupted by both of the liberals at once, who shouted about Hillary's superhuman achievements as a lawyer, humanitarian, and, let's not forget, as an author and "goodwill ambassador."

One challenged: "What about everything she's done for children?"

The conservative shot back: "Tell me, what? What, specifically, has she done for children?"

The other was momentarily taken aback. Everyone *knows* Hillary Clinton has done *loads* for children. "She's a child advocate," she said, belaboring the obvious.

"What's she *done*? She screams, 'I'm for the children, I'm for the children!' But show me one significant piece of legislation she has to her credit. Show me anything!"

Let's just say it did not end well – and I haven't even gotten to the part where one of the liberals talks about how FDR had lots of affairs, but no one ever threatened him with impeachment. . .

"But no one knew about FDR," you can hear Priscilla exclaim.

"What are you talking about? Of course they did!"

"The press, maybe, but they protected him."

"*Everyone* knew!"

As gasped the dying John Wilkes Booth, paralyzed by a shot through the spine and surrounded by enemies, after asking that his lifeless hands be held to his face: "Useless, useless. . ."

Friend or Faux?

THIS IS GOING to get personal. Then, again, when the subject is sundered friendship, what else could it be?

I used to have a good friend – let's call him Nick. A writer specializing in popular culture and politics, he was a lefty from way back – but, then, when we met, so was I. Though I was aware that he was somewhat baffled when I began my rightward drift, I was caught short – and royally pissed off – when a couple of friends in common reported he'd told them I'd changed only because I'd recently struck it rich with a book deal.

"Sure, I said it," he replied immediately, unembarrassed, when I called to demand whether the report was accurate. "I think it's true."

"What the hell are you talking about? A, I'm not making all that much from the book. And B, money doesn't have a damn thing to do with it!"

"Listen," he said coolly, in that smug, high-handed way of his that somehow had never bothered me before, the one that I'd come to associate with so many on the Left, "as far as I'm concerned, greed is the only reason anyone *ever* becomes a right-winger."

I guess there's something to be said for that kind of honesty, but nothing I was interested in. The friendship ended right there.

There's an aphorism attributed to Indira Gandhi that applies: "You can't shake hands with a clenched fist."

Talk to conservatives, especially those who started out on the Left, and you'll hear a lot of stories like that. "It truly is astonishing how few liberals credit those on the other side with having any principles or ideals worthy of respect," notes John Leo, the columnist, whose social circle includes many liberal eminences in journalism and the arts. "You can go your whole life and not hear a liberal take seriously any conservative argument – they just yell 'racist' or 'fascist' and think they've won."

True enough, direct attacks on one's very decency, like Nick's on mine, are hardly the norm; civility is the natural order of things and most of us are especially protective of our friendships. But with a certain kind of adamant left-liberal, the possibility of such an outburst is always there, lurking, lurking, and there's no telling what will set it off.

For Amy Anderson's impassioned, irrational, newly left-of-center friend Jane, the tipping point was *Fahrenheit 9/11*. "One night I'm in the kitchen, trying to get dinner on the table for the kids," recalls Amy, a good-natured, tart-tongued Westchester mother of two, "and the phone rings. She's just seen this ridiculous movie, and it's like the road to Damascus – she's seen the light! She starts haranguing me: 'How can you support these monstrous people? What is wrong with you?' Just this emotional *sturm und drang*, viciously attacking me, hammering and hammering away. This, mind you, from a woman who does not read the paper, does not listen to radio, someone not plugged in in any way. I swear to God, she didn't even know who Rupert Murdoch was! But we'd been close since college, she was my maid of honor and godmother of one of my children, and I wanted to save the friendship. So finally I said, 'Jane, stop, we cannot talk about this.' But, really, the damage had already been done."

For Marlene Mieske, a psychiatric nurse and reformed Sixties veteran, it was the right to bear arms that abruptly ended a friendship. "We'd always gotten along wonderfully, this woman and I, and just then we were co-chairing a blood drive. But it was shortly after Columbine and we were in New York City, so someone walked in with an anti-guns petition. Of course, everyone but me immediately signed. When I refused, this woman was beyond furious. Her attitude toward me changed *instantly* – it was literally as if she couldn't stand the sight of me, just stood up in a rage and started to leave. I said, 'Hey, hold on, wait a minute. Let's talk about this. You've got to understand that I grew up in the country, my father hunted, so to me it's okay – it's the Second Amendment, part of the Constitution.' She wouldn't even answer. And she never talked to me again."

Nor, she adds, was such a thing unique in her experience.

"The people I work with are very caring, but they're almost all liberals, and to them my beliefs are just incomprehensible. I'll never forget having lunch in the conference room of the Brooklyn Bureau of Community Service, right after Giuliani announced he was withdrawing from the Senate race with prostate cancer, and all these people, my *friends*, are going 'Yesss, Giuliani has prostate cancer! Isn't that the best news you've ever heard?' And I said: 'Tell me, how would feel if it were just announced Hillary has breast cancer?' They just looked at me blankly, and I said: 'Enough said.' From that time on, they never talked in front of me again. I was labeled – and it was my problem, not theirs."

"Another woman," she adds, "your typical major Upper West Side liberal, someone I've known for twenty-seven or twenty-eight years, actually said to me, 'Marlene, I know you've worked with the mentally ill, so I know you care about people. But how can you be a good person and a conservative?' It's sad – we've now reached the point where we really can't really discuss anything."

On the basis of my random survey, stories of friendships fallen victim to ideology are told by men and women in roughly equal numbers, but they tend to differ considerably in tone. We men generally dismiss our ex-friends, as Norman Podhoretz memorably dubbed his own impressive roster, with bemusement or contempt, identifying them as the jerks they are. "Every time the name Palin came up, his wife would start frothing at the mouth, and he'd follow right along" as one guy says of a recently jettisoned pal. "Why would I even want to stay friends with a wimp like that?" Another, thinking back on the Upper West Side parties he no longer attends, told me, "Every time I'd say to someone, 'No, I don't think all criminals are victims,' or 'Yes, I do think welfare does harm,' another jaw would drop, and someone else would accuse me of being a monster. After a while, my reaction became, 'Okay, fine, these people aren't my friends anymore. That's the way it is, and the hell with them.'"

But women, annoying as the fact may be to biology-be-damned feminists, are wired differently, and seem to feel these losses more keenly.

"There's no question my world has narrowed," as the Manhattan Institute's Kay Hymowitz puts it, with a note of at least quasi-regret, "and my social life has been greatly diminished. I actually used to stay up at night, thinking, 'I should've said this, I should've said that' – like the kid feeling left out. One old friend basically let me know she can't have me around anymore, just can't fit me in, because I supported the war. To her, conservatives are all Darth Vaders, planning mayhem and war for the fun of it. And this now included me."

All of which brings us back to the key question: Is it even possible to be genuine friends with someone who believes that you – or, if not precisely *you*, everyone who agrees with you – is a vicious, mean-spirited, greedy, bigoted s.o.b.? A bunch of liberal educators have actually created a scorecard that helps provide an answer to this question. Like most liberal initiatives, it is pitched to the mental/emotional level of your average six-year-old – the only difference being that, this time, six-year-olds were actually the target audience, the checklist having been created in reaction to the much ballyhooed "epidemic" of schoolyard insensitivity, once known as "childhood." Anyway, for our purposes it provides a handy means of grading the performance of our liberal friends in the plays-nice-with-others department.

This being my book, I will take the liberty of handing out the grades:

- Good friends listen to each other.
  Do yours?   *Grade:* F

- Good friends don't put each other down or hurt
  each other's feelings. Do yours?   *Grade:* D

- Good friends can disagree without hurting each other.
  Can yours?   *Grade:* C-

- Good friends respect each other. Do yours?   *Grade:* C-

- Good friends give each other room to change.
  Do yours?   *Grade:* F

Then again, who's kidding whom? It's not like such friendships have much of a payoff for those on our side of the fence, either. A casual bond with someone in the office or the neighborhood is one thing, sustained easily enough by the occasional give-and-take about the kids, or work, or the latest pop tart to disgrace herself publicly. But if you care as deeply as some of us do about the state of the nation and the culture, how do you remain tight with someone who quotes Keith Olbermann and Paul Krugman, or has no problem with campus speech codes, or can hear America compared to Nazi Germany and feel anything other than utter revulsion?

Old times' sake being the fine thing it is, we often find ourselves hanging on, even as the returns diminish with each awkward conversation. "The common ground just kept getting smaller and smaller," one woman says of a once-close friendship. "What to talk about became a real problem – because after a while, we couldn't even talk about pop culture or shopping without hitting a land mine."

"We still see each other on important occasions," says someone else, "but that natural give-and-take is gone, and it's all very superficial. How can there be a real friendship when you can never be honest or real?"

My wife and I know a couple, Paula and Alex, about which we feel exactly such a sense of loss. Paula and I were friends first, right out of college, when we briefly worked together, and when our respective spouses happened along, we clicked as a foursome. We had a great deal in common – including, back then, the usual gamut of liberal attitudes and assumptions – and over the years they've been kind and generous friends. We've spent innumerable pleasant evenings together, consulted each other regularly about life and careers, and watched one another's kids grow up.

At first, when we began to diverge politically, it didn't seem all that great a problem. Although outspoken about many things and given to hilariously blunt critiques of both the passing scene and many individuals in it, Paula had never been much interested in politics; her husband, while a liberal by birth and inclination, is a gentle soul, given to a bemused live-and-let-live-ism all too rare on the Left.

But at some point they got very chummy with a woman in their extended circle, a fairly well-known old-line feminist, someone who'd actually written finger-wagging books full of terms like "patriarchy," "heterosexism," and "hegemony." Paula, who'd always been blithely indifferent to the raging culture wars, suddenly started coming out with the most astonishing statements of her own.

I can nail almost precisely the time and place when it became clear that the friendship was in serious trouble. It was between 9:30 and 10:00 on a Friday night in February 2005, over dinner at a Japanese restaurant in Manhattan's West Twenties. Somehow, foolishly, we'd let the conversation wander onto the then-current firestorm involving Harvard President Larry Summers and his critics on the left, feminists and their pathetic male fellow travelers.

You'll recall that Summers had committed the unpardonable sin of free and open inquiry by speculating that one of the reasons more men than women are to be found in the upper echelons of math and the sciences might be innate differences between the sexes.

The moment Summers's name came up, Paula made clear that she did not regard his views as either commonsensical or in the spirit of free and open inquiry. "You know what I wish?" she asked, smiling, as if certain everyone present would agree. "That he would be reincarnated as a woman."

I caught my wife's look at that instant, and understood that we'd crossed a Rubicon; she may still have been fond of Paula, but I could see the respect melting away. There followed a brief, intense back and forth, in which we more or less made our feelings known, before both sides backed off in deference to our shared history.

But I know how we talked about that moment on the way home, and, knowing them, have little doubt about how they talked about us. As the philosopher Blaise Pascal once observed, "Few friendships would survive if each one knew what his friend says of him behind his back."

So, yes, I still have deep, deep affection for them. We still see each other from time to time, and are always careful to avoid land mines. But what mattered most, the ease that comes with the certainty of shared values, is irretrievably lost.

Only here's the thing: In recent years, individually and as a couple, we've forged a variety of new friendships. Just about my favorite few hours every month are the ones I spend over lunch with my fellow contributing editors at *City Journal*, the quarterly of the conservative Manhattan Institute, trading thoughts, kibitzing, and occasionally having at each other, on politics and policy. It's a great comfort to know that no matter how much we might disagree on waterboarding or the utility of vouchers, those differences pale beside our shared bedrock beliefs and principles. "That's the lifeline, people who are on the same page," Kay

Hymowitz, one of those new friends, sums it up, "people who don't make you feel" – she laughs – "*weird*."

"What really struck me is the intellectual environment I found on the right," adds Marlene Mieske. "I can sit around with other conservatives, and know that even if I say something they find outrageous, I won't be ostracized – I'm still family. As a former liberal, I can't tell you how refreshing that is."

What's especially satisfying, and more than a little startling, is how many of my oldest friends have made the same intellectual and moral journey from left to right as I have. Among these is a guy named Cary Schneider. We met way back in journalism school, when we were twenty-one – slightly younger than our sons, close friends themselves, are today. Cary and I talk at least three times a week, everything from baseball and work to politics and movies. Though there's a lot of kidding around, it is all undergirded, as it always has been, by a double-wide-load of common assumptions. Only now these assumptions have largely to do with the lunacy of our former creed, liberalism, and the incalculable damage it has visited upon the land.

My wife has a friend like that, too, a woman named Jenny, with whom she grew up in Northern California, and likewise went to Berkeley, moved east and, glory be, also ended up on the Right and largely isolated. She and her husband Gerry live in a small Connecticut town a couple of hours away, and late on Election Day afternoon, we drove up there to wait out the coming storm together. Except it never came – never, at least, penetrated the walls of their home. We sat up late before the fire, bellies full of braised short ribs and mashed potatoes, wine glasses in hand, talking, interrupted only occasionally by their teenaged son, who was monitoring the TV. Gloomy as his reports were, among such friends, things didn't seem nearly so cataclysmic. The women reminisced about the Monterey Pop Festival, where as teens they both worked shepherding zonked-out rock legends to their hotels; Gerry, who teaches English at an inner city vo-tech high school, told mesmerizing stories about his battles with administrators to teach Shakespeare instead of the Alice Walker and the rest of the P.C. crap on the approved list, and how, once he won, the kids blossomed in their belated exposure to the Bard.

Then, briefly, the spell was broken. "I already arranged to take a sick day tomorrow," said Gerry. "I knew I wouldn't be able to stomach the other teachers' gloating."

"Oh, c'mon," snapped Jenny. "Londoners survived the Blitz, we'll survive this."

"Gosh, Jen, I wish we lived closer together," cut in my wife, going sentimental. "You, us, Cary and Lucy, Kenny and Carol. . ."

"A commune!" Jenny laughed. "There's a hoary old idea that's come and gone."

"And maybe should come again, for conservatives, under Obama."

We all laughed. But at that moment, the idea didn't sound half bad.

Dinner Party Mischief

OR, HOW TO LOSE FRIENDS
AND INFLUENCE NO ONE,
BUT HAVE FUN DOING IT

SINCE THERE IS an approved left-of-center stance on everything
from taxing the rich (good) and nuclear energy (bad) to Jon Stew-
art (hilarious) and global warming (settled science; more proof of
humankind's awfulness; my God, what about the polar bear?!),
liberals always know exactly what they *should* think. The catch is
that there are certain issues on which, for many, the approved
position is quite a distance from what, privately, they do think.

This can provide all kinds of amusement for the enterprising
conservative at a neighborhood dinner party or barbecue.

For many years, the number one cause of liberal psychic disso-
nance was crime. Often the mere mention of an especially brutal
rape-murder by a recently paroled thug was all it took to set liberals
to disagreeing amongst themselves. Welfare – that is, its clear role
in promoting dysfunction – was also good. (Note: For maximum
effectiveness, it was important to use the term "well-intentioned"
in this context, since liberals like not only to be absolved of responsibility for their own foolishness, but also to be praised for it.)
Finally, for a time, before Bush Derangement Syndrome took
hold, there was 9/11.

These days, there is no issue more likely set liberals at each
other's throats than affirmative action, since most liberals know
as well as we do that racial preferences are a scam; the trick, given
their terror of being called racist, is getting them to say so. A
quick anecdote – say, about some local white kid whose doctor

mother happened to have been born in Argentina being admitted to Yale as an Hispanic – is often enough to get things rolling. With luck, one of them will bring up that, while Obama officially supports preferences, he doesn't want his own kids to benefit from them; and remind everyone of Martin Luther King's admonition that people ought "not be judged by the color of their skin but by the content of their character," so you won't have to – though it will almost surely be left to you to let drop that JFK abhorred racial preferences, whereas Richard Nixon supported them.

I'm proud to say that one evening, a couple years back, I actually helped engineer the following delightful exchange (dialogue not all that far from verbatim).

> ANGUISHED LIBERAL GUY: I'm just not sure it's right that the kids of this African-American lawyer I work with, who has more money than any of us, should get an advantage over the kids of a West Virginia coal miner.
>
> ME: Or the kids of Vietnamese boat people. [*Blank stares all around.*] Because, as I'm sure you know, Asians aren't eligible for affirmative action. They're classified as an "over-represented minority."
>
> ADAMANT LIBERAL WOMAN: Well, I'm sure there are problems, but black people still need it. It's their turn.
>
> ALG: That's easy to say, but what if it's some less qualified African-American kid getting a place at a college instead of your daughter?
>
> ALW: I'd want the African-American child to get the spot, so my child will personally experience just a tiny bit of the unfairness they've had to suffer for centuries.
>
> ALG (*disbelieving*): Right, let's talk again when *that* happens.

My favorite tale in this vein is from a friend of mine in the left-of-center bastion of Park Slope, Brooklyn. She reports creating not so much anger as level-red discomfort when the talk at a recent party turned to gay marriage. Everyone was for it, of course, including my friend, more or less. "But wouldn't it bother you if your own children were gay?" she asked, all innocent curiosity. "After all, isn't it natural to want your kids to mirror your experience? To have a traditional marriage and raise children in the traditional way? I can't think of anything that would make them more foreign."

She reports that, hearing this, the liberals around the table "got very flustered, because of course they feel exactly the same way. There was a long silence, and then someone said, 'I would be much more upset if my kids were Republican,' and that let everyone off the hook. But afterward, one liberal friend came and whispered in my ear, '*I* would be really devastated.'"

If You Can Take It Here, You'll Take It Anywhere

ONE INTREPID
NEW YORK CONSERVATIVE
REFUSES TO BEND OVER

IS IT POSSIBLE to find a single individual whose experience exemplifies the special scorn liberal New Yorkers reserve for their intellectual and moral betters on the right – one lonely figure who takes the worst they can dish out and never breaks a sweat?

After some thought, I came up with a number of plausible candidates. Perhaps an activist with the Catholic League, that perennial target of local Catholic bashers. Maybe one of the good folks at 1211 Avenue of the Americas, whose paychecks are signed by Rupert Murdoch. How about one of the band of intrepid military recruiters stationed in Times Square?

Then it hit me: a landlord!

Talk about having it tough in New York! Even more so than other places, the very word instantly summons up "cold," "heartless," "greedy," and worse. It is the landlord's lot to experience 200-proof, self-righteous New York leftism on a daily basis – even from non-lefties! In this respect, even my beloved *New York Post*, for all the full-blooded conservative politics of its opinion pages, is right down there in the gutter with the *Times*. Just a handful of pertinent *Post* headlines of recent vintage:

· "SLUM BUM" JAILED – LANDLORD FROM HELL

· LEAD PAINT LOUSE – KIDS AWARDED $21M

- RENT-FREE FORTRESS – TENANTS LOCK OUT LANDLORD
- BRAIN-DAMAGE TOT FACES EVICTION FROM ICY HOME
- GET LOST, GRANNY – LANDLORD BOOTING SENIORS
- SCAMLORD CAUGHT IN OWN 'NET
- LANDLORD: I KILLED MY TENANT

I approached a number of landlords who seemed responsible, with well-maintained buildings and nary a murder or brain-damaged tot on their resumes. No luck getting them to talk. To a man (and, in one case, woman), they were as cagey and paranoid as mob hit men. Even offered the print equivalent of dark glasses and phony beard, they were convinced they'd somehow end up with a liberal shiv in the neck.

Then I came across someone even better: a lawyer, Brad Silverbush, who represents landlords exclusively. Silverbush had no hesitation. When I turned on the tape recorder, it was as if I'd simultaneously hit *his* start button.

Remember Nick Naylor, the protagonist of the novel and movie *Thank You for Smoking* – the brilliant lobbyist for Big Tobacco who breezily notes that he's among the most despised people on the planet? Brad Silverbush is that guy, New York-style. Charming, plain-spoken, and, above all, thick-skinned, he knows he's fighting for truth, justice, and the American way, so couldn't care less that everyone he passes in the city's streets believes he's doing the devil's work.

As the son of a Holocaust survivor, he grew up thanking the fates for the privilege of living in this country, under the free enterprise system, and has liberals and their moth-eaten dogma pegged for exactly what they are. Sure, he acknowledges, there are some rotten landlords out there. But he also knows that the overwhelming majority of building owners do their jobs honestly and well, and, moreover, that if under Obama, the rest of America ends up embracing New York's entitlement mindset, we're doomed to turn into Bulgaria, circa 1962.

"Listen," he says, "you go out to Wyoming, or Virginia, or anywhere else where normal people live, and start telling stories about what goes on in New York, and they think you're making it up. If anyone tried to pull that shit where they live, someone would pull out a gun and – bam! – they'd put a stop to it." He laughs. "But in New York, it's the way it is, it's reality."

What "shit," exactly? "Say you're an average guy," he offers, "and you decide to buy a small building in New York City as an investment. Sounds good, right? Next thing you know, your tenants aren't paying rent, the city's treating you like garbage, and you're getting dragged before the Human Rights Commission because someone called you a racist – and nobody cares, because they think you deserve it."

Silverbush has lots of stories, full of horrifying particulars, and almost all of them in one way or another summon the same adjective: Kafkaesque.

But let him tell it:

The first thing anyone learns as a landlord is that in every situation he is presumed to be the bad guy. The evildoer. And everyone with whom he deals – his tenants, the city, the courts – is a potential enemy. I work with one guy, great guy, honest as they come, who runs a family business, a small company that owns and manages half a dozen buildings in Manhattan. I actually fear for him. Being a landlord in this city, putting up with the crap he has to, is literally driving him crazy. Not long ago he got a summons for a minor elevator violation in one of his buildings. It was a mistake – some bureaucrat had put down 2006 instead of 2007. So he's charged with being a year overdue with making the repair, which is a criminal violation. He can go to jail for this. But he's a trusting guy, so he goes down to Criminal Court, figuring he'll explain the mistake and that'll be that. Doesn't even bring a lawyer. Right, fat chance. There he is, surrounded by hookers and drug dealers, "mother rapers and father rapers," and they're all getting off with twenty-five-dollar fines. When it's his turn, the judge won't even listen to his explanation, just assumes he's a lying prick and starts threatening to throw him in jail! He ends up having to pay an $1800 fine – more than all the real criminals combined.

He pauses. "His crime was that he owned property in New York City."

That's how most of the Housing Court judges are – with only a couple of exceptions, maybe two out of twelve, just a real landlord-hating bunch. I had a case not long ago where we absolutely had the guy dead to rights. A dentist. He had an apartment on the East Side but was actually living across town with his girlfriend. I had testimony up the wazoo – I had the super, the managing agent, the doormen in both buildings, the mother of his child! But the judge, formerly a Legal Aid attorney, brushes it all aside with one sentence: 'I find all the landlord's witnesses not worthy of belief.' Boom, it's over. Even the tenant's attorney couldn't believe he won the case.

The former Legal Aid judges are the absolute worst. There's one whose husband is the head of criminal Legal Aid in Manhattan. How's that for a left-wing combo? Sometimes I just picture the two of them at dinner, sipping cheap wine and laughing at guys like me and my clients. I mean, these are people who never spent a day in the private sector in their lives, and just have real contempt for it. There's not even any pretense: the rules, the regulations, the law, everything's constantly open to reinterpretation.

I just had a case where the building had a firm "no pet" policy and this woman had a dog. The landlord wasn't unreasonable. He would've allowed it, but the woman was incredibly nasty and the dog was even nastier; it kept scaring little kids in the elevator. So what happens? The woman argues that she's entitled to "a reasonable accommodation," which is basically a regulation put in for blind people with seeing eye dogs. She proceeds to produce affidavits from psychiatrists saying she's depressed and needs a companion dog.

That's another problem, by the way – you can get a New York psychiatrist to testify to anything. I have a friend who represents a guy who hacked up his girlfriend, boiled her in soup, and fed her to homeless people. Every year he applies for release because he's gotten some psychiatrist to testify he's no longer a threat to society. That's a fun case. I go watch it whenever it comes up.

Anyway, the woman with the dog. Amazingly enough, in spite of everything, I win the case. But here's the sick thing: Even when the landlord wins, he loses. Because what does she do now? She files a human rights complaint against the landlord for failing to provide the reasonable accommodation for her dog!

Oh, man, the Human Rights Commission! Their hearing officers are even worse than the Housing Court judges. The assumption is that the landlord's done wrong – otherwise, why would you be there? So you walk in and all they want to talk about is how you're gonna make it right by this tenant.

It goes without saying that in New York, *everyone*'s a protected class – blacks, Hispanics, women, gays, the elderly, the infirm. One woman went to the Human Rights Commission claiming that my client was discriminating against her because she was a young, single woman. I can't tell you how many reams of documentation we had to file proving there were other young single women in the same building against whom he was demonstrably *not* discriminating – the difference being that those single women were actually paying their rent.

And try firing a lousy employee of the wrong ethnicity! One landlord had an alcoholic who never showed up for work, a Hispanic guy. After a hearing and arbitration, he had to pay to put the doorman in rehab, then rehire him. So the doorman goes back to work, and in a couple of weeks the same thing starts happening again, so there's another set of hearings and more rehab – all out of his pocket. No exaggeration, it took four years before he could finally get rid of him – with a year's severance.

Of course, there is a hierarchy of victimhood. Gay definitely trumps female and even elderly. I saw this firsthand with a case where a gay guy went up against a psychotic old woman. She lived below him and was making his life miserable, constantly complaining he was making too much noise – banging the ceiling with a broom or ringing his doorbell in the middle of the night. The gay guy was so terrorized that he was afraid to go to the bathroom at night and took a pee bottle to bed with him. So the landlord sides with him to try and get her out of the building. This miserable woman was no fool. She shows up in court with an oxygen tank, one of the huge ones, on wheels! Fortunately, we had one of the decent judges, a woman who knew bullshit when she saw it. Plus, the gay guy gets on the stand and starts crying. *Plus*, we had some terrific testimony from the previous tenant in the gay guy's apartment.

33

When he was up for a government job, she told the government interviewer he was a pedophile and a drug dealer. So we, the gay guy and the landlord, win the case!

But you think that's the end of it? The gay guy goes back to court demanding a rent rebate for all the time he couldn't make noise and had to pee in the bottle – and he wins! The landlord has to waive eight months' rent, in addition to paying the attorney's fees!

There's tons of people in New York trying to scam the system, and feeling completely justified about it. Why shouldn't they, when they're only screwing a landlord? The city's No Heat Line offers all kinds of opportunities for unscrupulous tenants – a quick call claiming inadequate heat, and an inspector shows up at the apartment and takes a reading. Tenants who are old hands at this just open up the windows before the guy arrives. The landlord gets a Class C violation – the most severe kind – and the tenant gets a rent abatement.

Anyway, it's not like the city doesn't do the same thing. Basically, as far as the city is concerned, the whole system is about one thing: making money for the city. They use this militia, inspectors, to go into buildings and look for violations. And if there's nothing there, they'll find something: a yogurt cup in the wrong recycling bin; trash cans put out too early; or the sanitation guys ripped open a bag and left stuff all over the sidewalk. God forbid there's a snowstorm and someone leaves a patch of ice!

As for tenants, if they're dishonest enough, it's almost possible to live in New York and *never* pay rent. Some of these cases drag on literally for years. There was one guy, a CBS sports producer, who wouldn't let anyone into his apartment to do repairs, then claimed he was living in a slum, and used this as an excuse to not pay rent for *six years!*

We're talking a two-bedroom apartment with a forty-foot terrace at Fifty-fifth and Sutton Place.

You soon realize that the people who yell loudest about other people's greed are almost always a lot greedier than the ones they're yelling about. They say it's hard to vote Democratic when you have a Republican lifestyle – not in New York. Because when you're a liberal in New York, no matter what else you do or how you behave in your own life, your politics make you a good person. I see it all the time. Someone'll lie, cheat, take advantage of people, but it doesn't matter, because supposedly the ends are right. It's a great moral racket they run.

In most of these cases, it's not like these people don't have the money. We're talking Wall Street guys, movie stars, people in television. The attitude in New York is that housing is a right. You shouldn't *have* to pay for it. I once had to evict Bozo the Clown.

Some of the most outrageous cases involve non-primary residence. I'm working right now with a landlord who has a woman with a very cheap rent-stabilized apartment. The woman lives in Greece – basically, she uses the apartment as a cheap hotel room when she's in New York. Theoretically, this is illegal, so when her lease expired, the landlord filed a non-primary-residence suit. Being in Greece, she kept filing for adjournments, until finally even the left-wing judge got fed up. For about five minutes, it looked like my guy might actually win – except now she's got it in the Court of Appeals and, of course, they keep giving her more time.

Does all this piss me off? Hey, if I let it, I'd be in a constant state of rage. Because, believe me, I am a certified expert on the breadth and depth and infinite variety of liberal hypocrisy in this city. But the only way to do it is to fight the bastards with everything you have, seeing them for what they are – and to keep your sense of humor. There's one landlord friend of mine who has it exactly right. I happened to bump into him right after he'd seen *Rent*, which at the time was being celebrated by every lefty in New York, and I asked him how he liked it. He gave me this long deadpan look, and said, *"Like* it? It's the musical version of the Bronx Housing Court!"

Kids in the Clutches of the Left

OR, HOW
GEORGE WASHINGTON CARVER
GOT TO BE THE FATHER
OF OUR COUNTRY

AT FIRST GLANCE, the story in our local weekly looked to be one those light features that serve as filler on a slow week. It was about the visit of an author to a nearby middle school – one Rosalind Wiseman, seen in the accompanying photo as a smiling, attractive youngish woman in a jaunty scarf.

But less than a paragraph in, the terrible truth became apparent. This was not the kind of visiting author many of us recall from our own school days back in the bad old days of the Fifties and Sixties, the sort who'd maybe read from her latest work of whimsical fiction or offer insights about some aspect of history or science stumbled upon in the course of research. No, the personable, thirty-nine-year old Ms. Wiseman had something entirely different in mind. She is the founder of a curriculum called "Owning Up," and goes around to schools explaining to kids "how power and privilege relate to unethical, cruel, dehumanizing and bullying behavior."

While the article is extremely enthusiastic about Ms. Wiseman and her work, embracing everything she says as gospel, sensible readers need only read the lines, not between them, to see that she is a prime example of the species *femina animosus*, trading in the hoariest and most pernicious of feminist clichés. "Men and women have to fit into boxes. . . . Men are supposed to be wealthy, athletic, strong, tough. . . . Society says girls are supposed to be pretty, thin, have nice hair (which usually means straight hair . . . a reflection of racism in the culture). . . . To the students' excitement, Wiseman showed them parts of a video by rap artist Kanye West called 'Stronger.' She analyzed the video showing them how it reinforced her box theory."

For these insights, the local PTA paid her $8000.

The day I read this, I happened to run across another school-related item on the net. Datelined Pelham, New Hampshire, it was about an unidentified woman who was spotted entering an elementary school, which set off a wave of panic reminiscent of Japanese monster movies. Convinced a mass murderess was on the loose, authorities ordered a security lockdown of not only the elementary school, but also the town's middle school and high school.

This, then, is where we stand in this country, child protection-wise, in the first decade of the twenty-first century. Where (as it turned out), a forty-year-old suburban matron needing to use the bathroom sets off heroic measures to safeguard children, a thirty-nine-year old leftist ideologue is welcomed into schools to preach a doctrine of pernicious politically correct crap that demands the abandonment of any semblance of critical thought.

Which brings us to a question with which countless conservative parents, especially those in America's blue precincts, are forced to contend: What to do about the relentless indoctrination that these days passes for enlightened teaching in our kids' schools?

Far too many of us have horror stories to tell about what our kids pick up, or fail to, in school. Nothing is too far-fetched or incredible. A woman from Brooklyn Heights told me that when she mentioned Martin Luther in a conversation with her thirteen-year-old daughter, an eighth grader in an expensive private school, she found herself haughtily corrected: "You mean Martin Luther *King*." A Manhattan father told a similar story about his fourth-grade son, the only difference being that the luminous historical personage in question was George Washington Carver, with the nation's first president in the role of his unknown predecessor.

Then there's "all that damn Native American stuff," notes my friend Kay Hymowitz, adding that in her Brooklyn neighborhood's schools, "it's like all of American history is the oppression of the Indians, followed by a two hundred years of nothing, followed by the Civil Rights movement."

Asked in a recent survey to name the most famous Americans in history, high school students awarded the top three slots to Martin Luther King, Rosa Parks, and Harriet Tubman – with the "people of color" parade finally interrupted by Susan B. Anthony in the fourth spot! "History as therapy," the writer Rod Dreher aptly calls it.

Would that the therapy were confined only to history. English teaching is arguably even worse. Conservative literary scholar Mary Grabar gives a whiff of what passes for critical analysis in high school English these days with a recitation of the textbook questions for student readers of Hawthorne's moving and morally complex classic, *The Scarlet Letter*: "How would you feel if you were Hester Prynne? How has our society changed? Aren't you glad that single mothers or sexually empowered women are no longer condemned?"

In fact, the obsession with race, gender, sexual orientation, and victimhood has migrated to every corner of the curriculum. In his splendid book *Breaking Free*, which deals with his own experiences as a New York City public school parent, Sol Stern tells of looking over his fifth-grade son's homework packet and realizing that it was "Christopher Columbus-bashing week" on the unofficial school calendar. He was not surprised to find a number of photocopied texts revealing Columbus as "a mean-spirited treasure hunter who brought pestilence and genocide to the innocent native population." But even he was taken aback by the week's math assignment:

Historians estimate that when Columbus landed on what is now the island of Hati (*sic*) there were 250,000 people living there. In two years this number had dropped to 125,000. What fraction of the people who had been living in Hati when Columbus arrived remained? Why do you think the Arawaks died?

In 1515 there were only 50,000 Arawaks left alive. In 1550 there were 500. If the same number of people died each year, approximately how many people would have died each year? In 1550, what percentage of the original population was left alive? How do you feel about this?

Of course, most liberals don't just *not mind* seeing their kids drenched in this multicultural idiocy, they *applaud* it, as yet another manifestation of their tolerance for those different from themselves. What a marvelous change this is, they will tell you, eyes aglow with the certainty of their own virtue, from the rah-rah Americanism that we had to endure in our dark-age school days. "You really can't even express any concern to them about any of this," as Hymowitz says of her Park Slope neighbors. "If you even bring up the obsession with race and the Indians – always the Indians! – you get this look of complete incomprehension. They *want* the teachers to be politically correct; that's what they *should* be. 'Traditional' is the curse word. No one wants to be seen as prudish or jingoistic or unhip."

In many places, the idiocy is so entrenched, so widely embraced as good and noble, that the very possibility of fighting it seems long since past. What can possibly be done about, for instance, the young social studies teacher from Vienna, Virginia, with a good three decades in the classroom ahead of her, who recently showed up as a contestant on "Jeopardy," telling Alex Trebek in the interview segment that in order to "inspire my students" and "celebrate diversity," she had fasted and studied the Koran during Ramadan?

40

Needless to say, the audience applauded. Also needless to say, some of us out there in TV Land rooted against this woman even more ardently than we do against the normal run of suspected left-wingers who turn up on the show – social workers, university professors, and the like – and, you'll be pleased to know, she was crushed. Still, it's not like this presents much of a strategy for dealing with the larger crisis.

So we get back to the question: How do those of us who know better see to it that our children are not corrupted by this stuff? How, as they head off to school to hear endlessly about America's alleged crimes and almost nothing of her glories, do we make sure they have a decent shot at seeing the world through, say, Bill Bennett's eyes instead of Bill Maher's? The estimable Mark Steyn put it best, as he so often does: "In the long run, the relativist mush peddled in our grade schools is a national security threat. But, even in the short term, it's a form of child abuse that cuts off America's next generation from the glories of their inheritance."

The easiest answer is the most obvious one: Keep them out of the clutches of these intellectual bomb throwers posing as educators in the first place.

Talking turkey – option one – there's home schooling, which has taken off in recent decades largely for this very reason. Conservatively, a word not chosen randomly, there are over a million kids currently being home-schooled in America, and most are thriving and then some, scoring higher than other kids on standardized tests, and succeeding to ever greater degree when they move on to college. Since there is no evidence that home-schooled kids are innately smarter, the academic benefits of learning at home seem beyond dispute.

I call this the Jeff Slater Effect. Jeff was a kid of altogether average intelligence and academic achievement with whom I attended elementary school. At the start of fifth grade, he came down with some dread illness and had to spend that whole year being taught at home. To everyone's astonishment, when he returned for sixth grade, he was a *genius*, revered by all for the range and depth of his knowledge. (This, plus the fact that he owned a rudimentary printing apparatus, induced me foolishly to appoint him head of my ultimately losing campaign for student body president.) Jeff's superior mental powers lasted only a year or so, at which point he fell back into the pack with the rest of us. But it is reasonable to speculate that, had his illness confined him to home his entire childhood, he might have remained a high achiever well into his twenties.

And yet liberals, as we know, urged on by their primo special interest group, the teachers union, have been trying to destroy the home-schooling movement, primarily through bogus claims that it facilitates abuse. Only "certified" teachers, they say, are up to the job of properly educating the young, an argument that was actually bought by the famously brilliant legal scholars of California's left-leaning Ninth Circuit.

Talk about a lame argument! Think back on some of the "certified" – and, in some cases, certifiable – teachers we public school vets endured during our educational careers. Or, by way of contrast, the kids we happen to know who have gone the home school route. My good friend Denis Boyles, the French correspondent for both National Review Online and this book, home-schooled three daughters with his wife April in locales ranging from Concordia, Kansas, to Tirana, Albania, with the result that the Boyles girls cumulatively have more knowledge than the leadership of the NEA and the judges of the Ninth Circuit combined.

Sure, lots of us parents have a problem with home schooling, but it has nothing to do with the nonsense put out by the teachers unions desperate to protect their incompetent own; it is that we ourselves are nowhere near up to the staggering task of serving as our kids' teachers. I mean, watching Denis and April work at it over the years, I can only marvel at their commitment. My wife and I, lacking that kind of follow-through, probably would've started with a rigorous regime of Greek and Latin, and ended up with several days a week mainly devoted to recess.

Then, for those able to afford it, there's the private school route. Not to say, if the issue is avoiding heavy-handed political correctness, that a private school or even a parochial school is necessarily the answer. "To some extent it's even worse," says one guy I know, who put his daughter in a New York Catholic school. "There are these horrendous courses in 'social justice,' basically teaching activism. The Berrigans are the model."

But going private, at least there's a shot. Take my friends, Rich and Martha, who live in that hotbed of left-wing conformity, Montclair, New Jersey. "The schools are the worst," observes Martha, explaining their decision, finally, to deplete their savings and go private. "They never stop preaching about 'tolerance' and 'diversity,' and there's not even the dimmest understanding how intolerant they are of any deviation from left-wing orthodoxy." They chose a place called Montclair Kimberly Academy, MKA for short. It had a reputation for rigor and respect for tradition, but who really knew? Then came their first parents' night. "I couldn't believe it," says Rob wonderingly, seven years later. "I'm looking around the classroom, and there are all these quotations on the wall, and there's one from *Edmund Burke!*"

But more typical is the story of a friend whose son attended the highly regarded Trinity School on New York's Upper West Side. "One day, we got a notice that there was to be some assembly where the point was to impress on the kids how great it is to be gay-lesbian-transgendered," he sourly recalls. "I immediately called the dean and said, 'I don't want our child to do this. It offends my standards, and I believe it is indoctrination.' It took some doing, but they finally gave in and allowed him to sit in his homeroom and skip 'Yippee, we're all gay' time."

He was lucky. I'll never forget receiving a similar notice from our kids' school, Fieldston, shortly after our daughter entered middle school. At twelve, she was tiny, and so innocent she'd only recently stopped half-believing in Santa, and here was the school notifying us that she had to attend a talk by a gay activist doing strange things with a condom and a banana. My wife, passionate by nature, and never more so than when the well-being of her kids is involved, raged into school the next morning to inform the dean that under no circumstances would our daughter be subjected to such a performance. Our daughter already knew plenty about the then-ongoing AIDS crisis – the disease had lately killed a close family friend, her brother's godfather – and we would get into the sexual particulars when we decided she was ready.

The dean was sympathetic but firm. She understood our concerns, but our daughter was part of the "community," and this was a community event. "You must remember," she added – and I trust you can imagine the condescending liberal sing-song – "we have scholarship students in this school who are sexually active at this age."

"You're not telling me you think that's appropriate?" countered my wife.

"Of course not, but it's reality."

"I see – so you're taking the aberrant and making it the norm." When the dean failed to answer, she added, "So, when are you going to start the free needle distribution program around here?"

Touché – and ill feelings all around. In the end, the woman wouldn't give an inch. Our daughter ended up attending the event, pronounced it "hideous," and went on from there. Still – and here's the point – we don't regret the effort, or the other such battles we'd fight in the years to come. We may not have put much of a dent in the smug self-certainty of this or that administrator or teacher, but they were not our only audience. Indeed, the lessons parents convey simply by fighting back are valuable beyond reckoning.

In my experience, no one has taken on the liberal educational establishment with more panache than Dennis Saffran, a lawyer from Douglaston, Queens, who has run for elective office as a Republican. As indicated by the following letter to his son's middle school music teacher, he brings to the effort just the right mix of civility, indignation and cool logic.

Dear Mr. ———,

I am very troubled to learn that you have again used your music class as a forum to impose a one-sided political lecture on the children in your charge. And I am especially troubled that in a discussion after class with my son, in the presence of several other students, you equated Republicans . . . with Nazis.

Let me begin by noting that one of my Nazi Republican views is a belief in student discipline and a corollary belief that, short of extraordinary circumstances, students owe their teachers obedience and respect. . . . I therefore recognize that [my son] is something of a flawed vessel for having to take on the daunting adult task of debating the teacher's politics – and for this reason I am all the prouder of him for having risen to this task.

. . . If you want to turn your class from a music class to a class on politics and current affairs, that's fine with me – though I suspect that most parents, as well as the school officials who eked out scarce budget dollars to pay the salary of a music teacher, would not agree. But if you're going to do this, then basic fairness and sound educational policy demand that you bring in another adult to present the other side of the issues to the children. Then the kids can arrive at informed opinions on their own. That's the American way.

In this spirit, I would be happy to come to your class to respectfully debate history and politics with you, or to invite a prominent moderate or conservative cultural commentator, such as John Stossel or Lynne Cheney (who, as you know, has authored a number of children's books) to do so. One topic for this debate might be your unchallenged assertion to the children that the big bad "red states" impose "one way of thinking" on their people. . . . If you think it would be unfair to ask you to debate a politically active lawyer or a prominent journalist or public policy intellectual – well, that's my point about the one-sided debate you're imposing on the kids.

Anyway, until we work out the terms of this debate exposing the kids to both sides of the issues, I would again respectfully insist as a parent that you please keep your political views to yourself and concentrate on teaching music – which from everything I've heard you do extremely well.

Then there was this one, to one of his daughter's teachers.

Dear Mr. ———,

We were very troubled to learn that our children were given an assignment to do a report on the music and culture of "the country where they're from," but that our daughter was told that she could not do the report on the United States.

Like so many children in this city and this country where various cultures have mixed and melded for years, our children do not have any single ethnic heritage. While it's really not anyone's business, their ethnic background happens to be part Irish, part Scottish, part German, part Swiss, and part East European Jewish. They have no idea which one to pick as their "cultural heritage," and forcing them to label themselves as one or another is both phony and a gross intrusion on our authority as parents to guide our children's cultural identity.

Finally, we think that it is particularly inappropriate at this time to attempt to divide the children of our school into "multicultural" boxes. The 350 firemen who died in the World Trade Center were not Irish-Americans, Hispanic-Americans, Italian-Americans, Polish-Americans, African-Americans, or any other kind of hyphenated Americans. They were simply Americans. Now more than ever, when our city and country are under attack, the school should be stressing the shared American culture that unites us. . . .

Has this head-butting with teachers done any good? As in our case, only in a few instances and over the very short term – i.e., no longer than it takes the teacher in question to get this trouble-some lawyer-parent out of his hair.

Nor does Dennis delude himself that these campaigns on his kids' behalf are without risk. "It's a fine line you have to walk," he observes, "because getting a reputation as the village crank or a right-wing rabble rouser isn't going to do my kids any good. On the other hand, they keep pushing that line further and further to the left, and you can't do nothing."

Even as he concedes that "my son hates for me to write these letters," he notes with considerable pride that at thirteen the boy is the opposite of a follower and often takes on these battles himself. "It isn't easy for him, but he does it. Even at his age, he understands about conformity, and sees that most people just don't want to go against the grain, and he decided he's not going to be that way."

It is a refrain that, in various permutations, you'll hear over and over again from conservative parents about their kids.

"My kids ended up with just a terrific bullshit detector," says Kay Hymowitz.

As soon as they hear the rote stuff about race, class, or gender, their ears perk up. In high school, my younger daughter was on the debate team, and one of the other kids, having read something I'd written, informed my daughter that I was a racist. I can't tell you how gratifying it was to hear my daughter stood up for me, and told him he was an asshole.

"My kids are more conservative than I am," notes Marlene Mieske, "and they learned it from experience. I'll never forget one of my sons coming home and telling me about a black girl he knew at school. He said, 'Mom, I was in half her classes, and she got Ds, and she got into Yale!' They grew up in a home where they were allowed to express those forbidden thoughts and develop their own very strong sense of personal integrity, and so they knew how to recognize *every* kind of injustice."

"There was an episode when my daughter was in eleventh grade that really made an impression on her," says another friend. "During a social studies discussion about abortion, she refused to go along with the crowd, and raised what she thought was the vital question of when life begins. The teacher went crazy, started ranting about how women had fought for this right for decades and only reactionaries felt otherwise. From that point on, this woman had a vendetta against her – personally blocked her from getting awards at graduation. But, you know what, my daughter is everything this awful woman supposedly wants a young woman to be – she's smart and capable and she's got backbone.

"I have three kids," he adds, "and they run from far left to conservative, with one in the middle. When we have other kids over for dinner, they're amazed. They're just not used to hearing conversations where there's disagreement and different opinions – yet no one's getting angry."

Alas, I must concede that my wife and I, as intemperate and bull-headed as conservatives as we once were as liberals, never pulled off that trick. Our daughter and son came to dread those moments when, with some pabulum-fed friend over for dinner, one of us would mock-casually seek to engage the friend in conversation on some political or social issue.

Nonetheless, inevitably, a great deal of it took. Now in their twenties, they're both powerfully independent-minded, about politics and everything else, and, really, there was never a time when they let even their strongest-willed teachers do their thinking for them.

I especially recall one episode back when my son was a high school sophomore. He had an English teacher, a white liberal, who began the unit on *Huckleberry Finn* by announcing that, although he was obliged to teach the book, he wasn't happy about it. It was a "racist" book, he said, the word "nigger" appearing with appalling frequency. There has, of course, been a lot of this lately. It is a measure of the times that Twain's masterpiece, famously cited by Ernest Hemingway as the progenitor of "all modern American literature" and among the most widely esteemed *attacks* on racism ever written, routinely appears on lists of works most aggressively under attack by book banners. These books are targeted, as columnist Michele Malkin succinctly observes, by those "too busy counting Twain's words to understand them."

It must be said that my son was both a highly indifferent student and a congenital wise-ass, so had very little margin for error grade-wise, let alone for rubbing teachers the wrong way. But he was already familiar with the Twain classic, so he raised his hand and protested that, in fact, it was an anti-racist book – indeed, one of the most powerful ever written. This launched an increasingly heated back-and-forth that he reported went on for a good ten minutes, culminating with the teacher's dismissive, "It's clear you have a lot of work to do on your racial sensitivity."

"Are you calling me a racist?" my son demanded, deeply aggrieved. When the teacher turned away, refusing to answer, he stalked out of class. He returned home from school that day, remarking: "Well, I'm starting out with a C in that class, and working down from there" – alas, a prophecy that proved all too accurate.

Some time later, I made the mistake of telling that story at the tail-end of a speech down in Texas, N-word included – I mean, that was the whole point, right? – and ended up getting in big trouble myself, branded a racist in newspapers throughout the state. But if I had the chance, I'd do it all again.

More to the point, I'm very proud to say, so would my son.

The WFB Memorial
Reading List for Kids

WHAT TO DO ABOUT
THE LIBERAL SCHOOL SYSTEM

THE ONGOING IDEOLOGICAL indoctrination of our children in their schools is one thing, and quite a gruesome thing at that. But it also goes on when they sit before the TV, or read many of today's children's books. For ours is a popular culture, also increasingly dominated by the left, that not only eschews brains and high culture in all its forms, but has discarded much that was best in shaping earlier generations of children in favor of P.C. junk. Where once most every child was raised with tales unapologetically drenched in lessons about good and evil – and, yes, as recently as the early Sixties, these were reinforced by TV shows, from "Gunsmoke" to "Leave It to Beaver" – the best millions of children get today is the banality of "Sesame Street", endlessly promoting the sort of "diversity" where no one looks the same and no one ever thinks differently.

Not even history books for children can be trusted these days. The wonderful Landmark series used to promote values like honor and physical courage with rip-roaring titles like *Custer's Last Stand*, *The French Foreign Legion*, and *Guadalcanal Diary*. Today's impostor of a successor Landmark series actually released a book entitled *Ain't Gonna Study War No More: The Story of America's Peace Makers*.

My wife recalls the moment when she realized just how bad

things had become. It was 1984. She was in our local library with three-year-old Sadie and infant Charlie, when she happened to pull down from the stacks Letty Pogrebin's *Growing Up Free: Raising Your Child in the 80s*. Leafing through it, she was transfixed with horror as one of the leading feminist lights of the day dismissed as twisted sexist propaganda the entire magical fairy tale genre. Through her feminist scrim, all Pogrebin could see was that "80 percent of the negative characters in the Brothers Grimm's tales are female." When she wasn't rooting out sexism in the library's card catalogue she was on the prowl for misogyny at the movies. *101 Dalmatians?* "Two unappealing female archetypes in animated dog and human form: simpering good wife and evil independent vixen." *Star Wars?* "All I saw was new weapons enforcing old power hierarchies, a simplistic polarization of good and evil 'forces,' and only two women: a princess and a housewife, the most reductive of all female sex role symbols."

What was so demoralizing was the realization that this drivel was already becoming mainstreamed and even institutionalized. "To reread this book now," as she says, "is to unearth, among other horrors, the first battle plans for the War on Boys."

We owe our kids so much more than that – owe them, to be precise, childhoods full of wonder and grounded in the wisdom of the ages.

What can parents do to help them get it? An excellent start, to paraphrase William F. Buckley Jr., is to stand athwart the encroaching popular culture shouting: "Stop!" Why feed them the moral and intellectual equivalent of junk food, when there's so much terrific time-tested stuff out there to nourish kids' minds, hearts, and imaginations? Most of it is readily available, and a lot cheaper, not to mention more effective, than anything to be found at the brilliant kids store at the mall.

What were some of the particular favorites in our family? With our kids now in their twenties, I put the question to my wife, who has a far better memory for such things. (I always find it easier to remember all we did wrong.) After brief consultation with the kids, she set down the following:

"I saw our job as steering between the Scylla of the P.C. Gestapo and Charybdis of the relentless vulgarity of popular culture. Since we were a mixed household – Harry loved history, baseball and Broadway, and I loved fiction, nature and opera – we competed to line up loyalists for our teams; with the result that our kids grew up with exposure to all those things.

"Of course, audio tapes were important – we're talking the days before CDs. When I'd drive Sadie to and from school, I'd stick my favorite cassettes in our Toyota's tape deck, with little Charlie strapped in his car seat as a truly captive audience. I still cherish hearing his two-year-old voice exclaim, after the final notes of the beautiful aria from *The Marriage of Figaro*, "Voi, che sapete," "Play it again, Mama!" (Alas, I've had to live off that thrill for twenty-one years; opera no longer ranks high among his varied musical tastes.)

"Another favorite was Ann Rachilin's Fun with Music series, wonderful stories told to all-time great classical hits. *The Man Who Never Was* (*Lieutenant Kijé*) and *The Secret of the Roman Pines* (Respighi's *The Pines of Rome*) were particularly beloved by our children. Then there was the Caedmon Collection of English Poets, featuring a very stirring rendition of Kipling's "If," read by Boris Karloff. Harry liked to weigh in on the history side – speeches by the likes of Churchill and JFK, Edward R. Murrow's "You Are There" recordings – as well as with old-time radio, notably Jack Benny.

"But of course the predominant influence was books," she says. What follows is her (very partial) list of the kids' early favorites.

SADIE:

· *A Doll's Christmas*, or anything else by the much-loved Tasha Tudor. Wonderfully matter-of-fact about dolls and their "world."

- The "Betsy and Tacy" series by Maude Hart Lovelace. The series takes the characters from age five to adulthood, the 1890s through World War I, and the prose level ages with them. A wonderful evocation of its eras, and characters who become lifelong friends.

- *An Old-Fashioned Girl* by Louisa May Alcott. Sadie loved all the Alcotts, but this was the series standout for us. The heroine, Polly, is a bit of a prig, but independent-minded and never swayed by the crowd or conventional ideas of popularity.

- *The Doll's House* by Rumer Godden. The same high standard as her adult novels. Not a trace of condescension.

- *The Wolves of Willoughby Chase* by Joan Aiken. The first (and best) in the terrific "Wolves" series, set in a fanciful version of eighteenth-century England and featuring high adventure, odious villains, and a pair of intrepid young protagonists.

- *A Little Princess* by Frances Hodgsen Burnett. Nothing better evokes Victorian London – or grit and perseverance. Still one of the best heroines around.

- The Blue, Red, Green, Yellow, Brown, Grey, Pink, Crimson, Olive, and Violet Fairy Tale Books by Andrew Lang. The best fairy tale collection going. Exhaustive.

CHARLIE:

- *The Jack Tales*, edited by Richard Chase – a wonderful collection of oral tales handed down by Southern mountain farmers, featuring a boy named Jack and his two brothers, Will and Tom.

- The "Penrod" books, by Booth Tarkington. Charlie's absolute favorite. Funny, smartly written, and as accurate a

depiction of eternal American boyhood as you'll ever find
– not to mention completely un-P.C.

· *Animal Farm*, by George Orwell, which was read aloud to
him by Harry when he was ten.

· *The Tomten*, by Astrid Lindgren, of "Pippi Longstocking"
fame. The Tomten is a gnome who lives on a farm and
watches over the entire family at night.

· *Thirty Seconds Over Tokyo*. Part of the original Landmark
series, the thrilling story of Doolittle's raid by one of the
participating pilots.

· The "Sherlock Holmes" stories.

· Mark Twain's short stores.

ENJOYED EQUALLY BY BOTH:

· The "Tim" series of picture books, set in England, written
and illustrated by Edward Ardizzone. Ardizzone puts his
young protagonists in all sorts of adventures, often on the
sea. There's a terrific five-year-old character named Char-
lotte, who is introduced to the series when she is saved
from a shipwreck and must earn her passage as the ship's
cook.

· The "Little House" books by Laura Ingalls Wilder.

· The "Moomin" books by Tove Jansson, a Finnish writer.
A delightful series about creatures called Moomintrolls.
Our children – and their friends, who discovered the
books through them – simply loved these books.

· *The Oxford Anthology of Poetry for Children*. Lots of great
ballads. "Admiral Benbow" was a particular favorite, along
with some Scottish poems written in broad dialect.

· *David Copperfield*. Their favorite among all the Dickens.

· The Bobbs Merrill Childhood of Famous Americans series. There are dozens of them, all terrific, but the best are the earliest, from the Forties and Fifties. Among them: *Babe Ruth: Baseball Boy*; *Buffalo Bill: Boy of the Plains*; *Betsy Ross: Girl of Old Philadelphia*; *Babe Didrickson: Girl Athlete*; *David Farragut: Boy Midshipman*.

· Horatio Alger's books. The tales of rags-to-riches through honesty and diligence inspired a century ago and they still do. Our kids also loved an Alger knock-off called "Tom the Telephone Boy." Between the lines, they're also terrific history lessons about that period in America's past.

An Exciting, High-Profile Career in Journalism!

BACK IN 2002, I spoke at a conference put together by the Inter-collegiate Studies Institute, which provides training and support for conservative college journalists. The kids were an impressive lot: young, eager, and, in more than a few cases, talented. But I wasn't quite sure how to answer the question that many of them kept asking: How can I get a job at (pick your poison) *The New York Times*, or in network news, or at *TIME*, or with any of a half-dozen other mainstream outlets on the elite list?

Of course, I understood. These are the media with which they grew up; maybe there had been a particular reporter or two who'd caught their eye and drawn them toward the profession. Many years before, for me, it was the distinguished-looking guy standing in the middle of the Champs-Élysées in a trenchcoat, the Arc de Triomphe looming behind, giving the latest news from war-torn Algeria – and always concluding with, "Peter Kalischer, CBS News, Paris." For a thirteen-year-old history buff and news junkie in the New York suburbs, this was the ultimate in grown-up existence: getting to write the first draft of history, followed by dinner at Maxim's and who knew what else!

I ended up giving the young aspiring journalists a semi-stiff dose of the truth, as I see it. Success at that level is tough even under the best of circumstances, I cautioned, and their politics would likely make it that much harder. In fact, they'd probably be wise to keep that aspect of themselves fairly tightly under wraps. Still, not being entirely heartless, what I didn't say was: *Be careful what you wish for.*

While I hadn't been starry-eyed about journalism for quite a while, I happened to be feeling especially cynical just then. This was the result of another gathering I'd attended down in sunny St. Petersburg, Florida shortly before the ISI confab, courtesy of an outfit called The Poynter Institute.

Poynter fancies itself an ethics institute for journalists, the sort of place that's always holding seminars on subjects like unnamed sources, and whose faculty members are constantly being quoted in the press in its bottomless fascination with itself. I was there for the annual meeting of Poynter's Board of Advisors, a collection of prominent journalists – in fact, exactly the sort of people for whom the young conservatives hoped to work. I, a non-prominent journalist, had been shoehorned onto the Board in a nod to diversity, the diversity having to do less with my non-prominence than the fact that I was the only quasi-conservative within miles of the place. Diversity is a huge deal at Poynter; it's the subject of many conferences and seminars – the word seems to pop out of someone's mouth every thirty seconds. Still, they paid all my expenses, plus a small yearly stipend, and fed me well. I can think of far worse places to spend a winter weekend than St. Petersburg.

But then, on the morning of the second day – trouble. The faculty and trustees had gathered, along with us Advisors, in one of those large, tiered classrooms, so that everyone could hear the Board of Advisors' take on the STATE OF JOURNALISM. Everyone was keenly aware of the fact that mainstream newspapers were increasingly unprofitable, and the question on the floor was: why?

The guy running the session went around the room, posing the question to each Advisor in turn, and things were said, and repeated, about the aging of the audience, rising paper costs, and the pressures exerted by broadcast media. The Internet was also mentioned a couple of times, but only in passing, since it was still fairly young and no one in this room of old-media heavyweights seemed to grasp the magnitude of the threat.

Then it was my turn. So I brought up what, in my circle, was patently obvious: A lot of people had stopped reading the goddamn paper because they were sick to death of seeing their most fundamental values and beliefs mocked and belittled on an almost daily basis! I was maybe four sentences into a considerably more polite version of this, when, from a couple of rows behind me, there came a booming voice: "That's a load of crap!"

It was Howell Raines, a fellow Advisor and at the time the executive editor of *The New York Times*. Journalists are power groupies, and at Poynter, Raines, a strutting, self-important bully then at the center of the journalistic universe, was revered, even if he was not much liked. Just the evening before, he'd been honored by the senior faculty – make that *fawned over* – for the *Times*'s 9/11 coverage, which had lately garnered a record number of Pulitzers.

Now the place seemed paralyzed, as he roared on about my colossal gall in making such an outrageous charge. Here I was at Poynter – *Poynter!* – parroting the bullshit usually heard only in the organs of the extreme right-wing fringe from reactionary malcontents!

Fortunately, I'd spent an entire childhood arguing with a pair of brothers, one of whom grew up to be a lawyer. When he paused for breath, feeling oddly calm, I replied simply, "That's not an argument, Howell, it's just name-calling."

"What name did I call you?" he shot back, going red.

"You basically said I'm part of the lunatic fringe."

As it happened, I was aware that my friend Bernie Goldberg's book *Bias* was making its initial appearance atop his own paper's Nonfiction Best Seller List the very next day. I noted this, pointing out that a lot of people out there certainly seemed to agree with the premise. This only enraged him further. "I'm very happy for your friend Goldberg," he spat sarcastically. "I'm sure he'll make a lot of money. That's the whole point, isn't it? What he wrote is crap, and he knows it."

"I think if you talked with him, or bothered to read the book, you wouldn't say that."

"I wouldn't touch that piece of trash. The man's an embarrassment to our profession!"

It is, of course, vital in such a situation to keep one's cool, and, Obama-like, I gave every appearance of keeping mine. But my stomach was churning, and my mind racing: *What an asshole! My God, what hell it must be to work for a guy like this! To so much as broach a dissenting opinion would be career suicide!*

We went back and forth a good five minutes, until there was nothing much left to say. Or, if there was, from my perspective, there clearly was no point in saying it. Because here's the thing: In that room packed with big-time journalists, no one else joined the fray. The way heads were turning, his way and then mine, it might as well have been a tennis match. Either these dunderheaded liberals agreed with Raines that the bias issue was completely unworthy of consideration, or they were so terrified of the big cheese from the *Times* that they wouldn't cross him in public. Or, quite possibly, both.

Whatever the case, the hell with them, too.

So I was surprised, at a luncheon immediately following the session, when a couple of my fellow Advisors approached me with consoling words. I was especially struck by the warmth of the editor-in-chief of the *Chicago Tribune*. "He won't be here next year," she whispered, referring to the fact that Raines's term as an Advisor was coming to an end. "So we can have a real discussion about this then."

This is what passes for courage in the wide (yet exceedingly narrow) world of mainstream journalism. If they ever had that discussion – and I wouldn't recommend holding your breath – it was without me. When the Powers That Be at Poynter asked me to re-up, I politely declined.

* * *

Journalism is hardly the worst field in which a conservative can find himself – check out the next chapter – but it is surely among the most frustrating. For it is a profession grounded in the fundamental yet zealously defended fiction that its ultimate values are objectivity and fair-mindedness.

In fact, in this sense, Howell Raines was actually better than most. He was an unapologetic left-liberal partisan, and hardly bothered pretending otherwise. In my admittedly limited exposure to Raines at Poynter, the only issue on which I ever heard his mind slightly open involved the possibility that Alabama might be unexpectedly competitive next season.

Yet what's telling is that his biases had nothing to do with his fall from power. His viciousness did. His own newsroom despised and feared him, and when the Jayson Blair fiasco left him vulnerable, they turned on him with the herd-bravery of the conspirators who cut down Julius Cæsar. In fact, in his wake, the *Times* is arguably more agenda-driven than ever, and, as always, the rest of the media trails eagerly behind.

As always, they heatedly deny the fact. Engage almost any mainstream journalist in conversation and see for yourself. Hell, get a group of them together. They'll scoff at the very suggestion, bat away every example, and then offer up definitive proof of their remarkable evenhandedness. Aren't they, after all, attacked from both the right *and* the left? If both sides are seeing bias, they're clearly playing it right down the middle!

On second thought, don't bother. It'll only drive you bonkers. While logic and the facts are on your side (do they actually *believe* the lunatics at Daily Kos and MoveOn.org have as much credibility as sources as senior military commanders and elected Republicans?), they'll never see it. Ever.

Of course, unlike me, liberal journalists have no trouble figuring out what to tell eager young people seeking their advice. At places like my alma mater, Columbia Journalism School, the message is as straightforward as it is uplifting: Go forth and change the world. And, no, by "change," the liberal journalists don't mean streamlining the tax code, or rolling back hate speech laws, or otherwise getting the government or multicultural zealots off our backs. Rather, they're urging the next generation of journalists to use their computers and cameras to "help the disadvantaged," "root out corporate corruption," "save the environment," and otherwise make careers of helping the likes of Barack Obama do the Lord's work.

After all, isn't this how the self-reverential Sixties vets now running the journalistic show have always seen themselves? "It is so hard, I think, for young people we know who work here at CNN and other news organizations to even imagine what Watergate was like," rhapsodized CNN anchor Judy Woodruff not long ago, thinking back on the work she and her contemporaries did in their glorious youth on the story that, whatever its other qualities, also sowed widespread cynicism and undermined the nation's faith in essential democratic institutions. "To have a White House come undone, an administration come undone, because of some news reporting!"

It is not that an occasional conservative won't sneak through the cracks. If you imagine the universe of contemporary journalism as a big "Where's Waldo?" tableau, he'd be the little guy by the water cooler in the lower right-hand corner, trying to pass as invisible. Needless to say, his presence has no effect on the attitudes and values that prevail in the place.

"I was not nearly as conservative at the time as I am now," says Clifford May, of the decade he spent as a reporter at *The New York Times*, "but I was still too conservative – so I kept it in the closet as much as possible. I tried never to talk about my political opinions, which naturally people on the left never feared to do. If you were gay, that was okay; if you were a Communist, that was all right. But you couldn't be a conservative."

"If you have conservative ideas of any kind, the first time you articulate it, you're marked," adds my friend John Leo, who worked for thirteen years at *TIME* before moving on to *U.S. News and World Report*. "It'll come up in some form or other if you want to get promoted. The only way around it is to become a *former* conservative – they like that. I know two or three people who did that, managed to de-louse themselves, and they now have big jobs in the mainstream media. To media liberals, that's even better than having been a liberal all along."

Bernard Goldberg was fortunate enough to have a different experience at a mainstream outlet, at least for a time. While his growing skepticism about the liberal worldview at CBS increasingly put him at ideological odds with his colleagues at the network, he had a boss who understood the value of his contrarian perspective, and this afforded him some protection. He was thus able to pursue stories other reporters not only weren't interested in, but couldn't even see. "I did a number of pieces on father's rights, for instance – not from a crusading perspective, but because they were great stories," recalls Goldberg. "I mean, there were guys out in California having to pay child support because they had similar names to the real deadbeat dads. I had a female lawyer tell me a woman would have to be caught in bed with her boyfriend, both of them drinking beer, for her to lose custody of the kids. This was important stuff, and no one else on TV was doing it. It wasn't conservative journalism, it was honest journalism."

Still, when one of his pieces raised uncomfortable questions about that liberal holy of holies, feminism, all hell broke loose. "It was on Christina Hoff Sommers's book *Who Stole Feminsm*, which exposed all the phony feminist statistics that said men beat up women in record numbers on Super Bowl Sunday, and that the biggest cause of birth defects is men roughing up their pregnant wives, and all kinds of other bullshit. Before it aired, [CBS News President] Andrew Heyward was in a frenzy. He went through that piece not just with a fine-toothed comb, but with an *electron microscope*. I was getting questions like, 'Well, then, what *is* the worst day, when *do* they get beaten up the most?' I said, 'How the fuck do I know? I didn't make up these ridiculous stories, they did!' At the same time, people were putting the most liberal, conservative-bashing stuff on the air every day of the week, and no one gave a damn!"

A mere couple of years later, Goldberg's independence of mind famously caught up with him, when he did an op-ed piece for the *Wall Street Journal* citing the bias at his own network. His career at CBS effectively ended the morning it appeared.

Quite simply, the mainstream media constructs a narrative on every major issue, and it's the very rare story that fails to adhere closely to the script. Feminists are the good guys; they fight for justice and a better, more equitable America. Global warming is "settled science" and a looming disaster. Tax cuts only help the rich. The war in Iraq was a horrendous mistake, and has made us less safe, so that assumption must remain front and center even when the war seems to be going well. And, yes, "bias" is a product of right-wing paranoia.

It's their story and, no matter what happens, they're stickin' to it. Witness the *Times*'s unchanging take on the sharp, decade-long drop in crime: In 1997, the headline: "Crime Rates are Falling, but Prisons Keep on Filling." In 2004: "Despite Drop in Crime, an Increase in Inmates."

As vital as *how* the news is covered is what *never* gets covered at all: generally speaking, almost anything that seriously challenges prevailing left-of-center orthodoxy on the environment, the war, affirmative action, or favored political figures. Indeed, Barack Obama's tight relationship with the poisonous Reverend Jeremiah Wright was being discussed on conservative web sites for a full year before the mainstream was forced, thanks to the videos of Wright's inflammatory sermons, to accord him serious attention; never mind that Obama had sat in Wright's church for twenty years, the media was instantly ready to accept his assurance it was all news to him. Then there's Juanita Broaddrick – the Arkansas woman who made a highly credible rape charge against Bill Clinton at the height of the impeachment brouhaha. Today, mention her name to even a well-informed liberal and you're sure to get a blank look, so complete was the media's blackout of the story that would likely have finished Clinton off.

"At *The New York Times*," says Clifford May, "my story ideas were often different from other people's, and my editors made clear that they weren't good ideas. Once, when I was correspondent in Africa in the mid-Eighties, I proposed a serious piece about Islam, one that would have been way ahead of the curve, pointing out that all Islam's borders are bloody. Their answer was a flat, 'No! Don't even think about it.' Another example: When I came home and was working in Washington, I was quite amazed and encouraged to see how well the Ethiopian community was doing. Someone would buy a taxicab, and in a few years they'd have a small fleet. They'd work anywhere, save their money and prosper. This to me was an interesting story. What are they doing differently from so many inner city blacks that they can come here, not speaking the language, and succeed? The answer was: 'That would definitely *not* be an interesting story. What makes you think we would want to do a story like that?'"

Eventually, says May, today an outspoken public conservative, "there reached a point where, between the frustration about what they wouldn't let me do and the general animosity toward conservatives, I knew I couldn't stay at the *Times*. I think this is the experience of all conservatives over there." He begins ticking off the names. "Richard Bernstein, John Corry, Michael Kelly, Hilton Kramer, of course. At a certain point, it's just too much." He laughs. "Not that I think I'm missed. I think it's fair to say most of my former colleagues at the *Times* look upon me the way assistant DAs look upon one of their number who's gone to work for the mob."

John Leo, now a senior fellow at the conservative Manhattan Institute, readily agrees about the importance of being able to walk around in one's own ideological skin. "Not long ago I was at a gathering with John Stossel and Myron Magnet and two or three others, and I looked around and said, 'Holy smoke, everyone here is conservative!' It was great! Suddenly you could have a free conversation without worrying about a pie flying in your face.

"People used to always write me saying, 'You have a lot of courage, you don't care what happens to you. I'd say, 'Look, it's easy to get accused of bravery when you're in your late sixties. I wonder what I'd do if I were twenty-three years old and just starting out in journalism. Because you can get squashed early, before you even have a foothold in the profession."

He's right. Still, the dilemma isn't quite as wrenching as it was a mere handful of years ago, because the media itself is in the midst of such dramatic and, for conservatives, heartening change. Readers and viewers continue to flee traditional outlets, and their once-vaunted reputations for fairness and probity are further shredded by the week. Conservative journalists have new options, in right-of-center publications, on FoxNews, on talk radio, and on the web.

Just recently, roaming online, I came across a young conservative writer named Ashley Herzog, identified as a journalism major at Ohio University. Her stuff was terrific, dealing with subjects like gun control, absent fathers, and the sexualization of young girls. Indeed, she could have been one of those kids back at ISI.

I especially liked a piece she did on the hypocrisy of the leftist icon Arthur Miller who, according to recent revelations, long ago fathered a son with Down Syndrome, whom he referred as a "mongoloid" and consigned to a mental institution. Starting with Miller, whose "pompous liberalism has been forced upon high school and college students ever since he wrote *Death of a Salesman* in 1949," young Herzog moved on to those other moral exemplars of the left, Rousseau and Marx, noting how, notwithstanding their treatment of people in their actual lives, they, like so many leftists, are seen as good and decent merely by virtue of their politics. "Is it just me," she asks, "or does there seem to be a correlation between radical socialist views and heinous personal conduct?"

"I think I have a lot to say," she asserts, with impressive self-assurance, when I track her down, "and I want to be able to say it." She tells me that, at twenty-one, she's already been hit with the epithets that lots of us dodged well into our forties – "fascist," "Hitler," "the devil" – so that part of it doesn't faze her a bit. Ideally, she'd like either to write books or do a syndicated newspaper column, since she regards Michelle Malkin as a model.

"No interest in working for a major paper?" I ask. "The *Times* or *Washington Post?*"

There's a pause, then, on the other end of the phone, she laughs. "Why would I want to? I think you'd almost have to be a masochist."

In Sarah Palin's Shoes

A HOW-TO FOR GETTING SMEARED

OF COURSE, far worse than being a conservative marooned in a mainstream newsroom – hey, at least one can always quit! – is being a conservative public figure at the mercy of the press.

Ask George W. Bush. Or Sarah Palin. Or whoever the Republicans end up nominating in 2012.

Hell, ask almost anyone in America with a marginally open mind. Simply by watching, listening and reading, most of us know exactly how partisan many reporters are.

As for me, after more than thirty years in the journalism biz, I thought I knew all there was to know about the way liberal journalists slant things, even as they delude themselves they're being even-handed, and how readily they'll smear those on the other side.

But, truly, I had no idea, *none*, until it happened to me.

To be sure, mine was a small-time case, a kind of mini-smear. Perpetrated in Texas, it never made national headlines. Still, trust me, it was a gruesome thing to go through.

Remember that episode I mentioned about my son and his argument with his teacher about *Huck Finn*? As it happens, I was doing a fair amount of public speaking back then, following the publication of my book recounting my move to the right, and in early 2002, I received an invitation from a Dallas-based group called the National Center for Policy Analysis. By now I had worked up a solid twenty minutes or so on the subject, a balance between personal anecdotal stuff and ruminations on the state of the culture and republic, and it had always gone over well.

Thus it was that I found myself that early afternoon in the

auditorium of the Federal Reserve Bank of Dallas. At the pre-speech lunch, I was seated beside the individual responsible for my being there, a most agreeable guy named Bob McTeer, president and CEO of the Dallas Federal Reserve. As McTeer explained in his introductory remarks, he'd run across my book by chance, found it amusing and provocative, and thought I'd have some interesting things to say.

He didn't know what he was getting himself into any more than I did.

As always, I began by reading from my book's back cover a list of "How to Tell if You've Joined the 'Vast Right-Wing Conspiracy'" – things like:

· "You're actually relieved that your daughter plays with dolls and your son plays with guns."
· "You sit all the way through *Dead Man Walking* and at the end *still* want the guy to be executed."
· "At your kids' back-to-school night, you are shocked to discover the only dead white male on your tenth-grader's reading list is Oscar Wilde."
· "And by the end of the night you realize the only teacher who shares your values teaches phys ed."

These got the usual laughs and some nods of recognition, and I moved on to the meat of the talk. I described my hard-core left-liberal suburban childhood, how I grew up hearing of the heroics of the Abraham Lincoln Brigade and rooting for sports teams based on how many blacks were on the roster; how, in college during Vietnam, my fellow student journalists and I, utterly certain of our own rectitude, cavalierly turned the school paper into a vehicle for New Leftism; and how, a few years later, views intact and the opposite of repentant, I was able to move seamlessly into mainstream journalism.

As was the case with so many others, I began to rethink things seriously only after I became a parent. I described how, in my case, the pivotal event was my wife's decision to stay home with our baby, a choice all but unheard of in our circle of driven New York professionals, full of feminist moms spouting the then-prevailing wisdom that day care was actually best for infants. So when my editor at *Esquire* wondered if I might want to contribute to the magazine's upcoming issue on women, I suggested a piece that would examine those assumptions, based on interviews with prominent pediatricians and child psychologists. In retrospect, the resultant piece was pretty mild, doing little more than posing questions about the possible long-term effects of early day care, but instead of bringing about the meaningful conversation I'd expected, the article prompted a ton of mail denouncing me as a vicious woman-hater.

I told the Dallas audience that this experience proved only the first in a series of eye-openers about the degree of intolerance of the ostentatiously tolerant when it came to dissenting ideas on key social questions touching on race or sex. The fact that these are precisely the issues that most cry out for free and open debate seems to matter not at all. In the increasingly illiberal world of orthodox liberalism, competing ideas are answered not by argument but by a pose of moral superiority and by-the-book invective. In the end, this is the ugly, destructive essence of political correctness: It undermines the robust back-and-forth so essential to the democratic process.

I concluded the speech with the story I mentioned earlier about my son and his white liberal English teacher, and her reluctance to teach *The Adventures of Huckleberry Finn* because it was "racist," the word "nigger" appearing with appalling frequency. I described the heated exchange between my son and his teacher and, yes, the pride I felt for his daring to stand up on principle to an intimidating authority figure. That concluded my talk. I got a round of applause and waited for questions.

Immediately a black guy in the middle of the room stood up. Later identified as William Jones of the San Diego-based CityLink Investment Corporation, described in a Fed press release as "an enterprise that acquires, develops, and manages real estate ventures and helps to renew urban areas," he announced that he didn't have a question, but a statement. He said he was "very personally offended by your jokes about black people and your seemingly rationalizing the use of the word 'nigger.' I'm a businessman, my wife is a prosecutor, my children go to college, we pay our taxes. The overgeneralization doesn't really help to further what I think you really want, which is understanding."

I stood there for a moment at the podium, stunned, not know-ing how to respond. I hadn't the slightest idea what I'd said to provoke such a response. *Told jokes about black people?* Not only had I not even remotely done such a thing, the suggestion that I ever would was beyond outrageous. *Rationalized the use of the word "nigger"?* I was describing what had happened between my son and his teacher. It was the word Twain used, what the two of them were arguing about – the very point of the story!

Then again, the tenor of his comment suggested that he perhaps hadn't even really heard what I was saying, beyond the offending word. Or that if he had, what he truly found so distasteful was a discussion of race that, since it challenged liberal verities, struck him as both unfamiliar and deeply unsettling – and was therefore far easier to tag as "racist" than to confront with argument.

But something else was at play here: As the brilliant black social critic Shelby Steele observes, there is in this country a pervasive "adherence to good racial manners," which dictates, among other things, that on matters of racial sensitivity blacks hold the moral upper hand, and that even when whites feel themselves blameless, the appropriate response to such a challenge is to defer, retreating in sober self-reflection, if not outright apology. In fact, for an increasing number of us, this is a key part of the problem – and one that should be called by its rightful name: condescension. Far from helping us address the many morally complex and deeply divisive issues involving race, it has the opposite effect of silencing those who question the liberal orthodoxy and otherwise cutting off meaningful dialogue.

I certainly had no intention of being confrontational, but I am not a racist and wasn't about to back off from anything I'd said. After a moment's hesitation, I replied that race was obviously a complicated and highly charged issue, but that it was one I thought essential to deal with openly and honestly. And while liberal voices tend to dominate the conversation, there were other voices that also needed to be heard more widely, ones that might take us beyond the familiar formulation of black victimhood and white guilt. For instance, perhaps he might look into what such black neocons as Shelby Steele, Thomas Sowell, and John McWhorter had to say on the subject. That was it. Unsettled as I was, I thought my response was more or less on point. After a few more questions, the Q&A session ended. I autographed some books, including McTeer's, posed for a few photos, and, running late for my plane, made a dash for the exit. On the way out, a young woman from the NCPA intercepted me. What that guy had said was awful, she said, bristling. He was part of a contingent from the San Francisco Fed, and it was as if he hadn't heard a word I said.

Well, I offered, people out in that part of the world do tend to be so marinated in P.C. that they often find different ideas deeply shocking. I joked that it was just lucky I'd had the presence of mind not to include another of my "How to Tell" observations: "Someone's going on about how fantastic San Francisco is, and it suddenly hits you that's the one place on earth you never want to live."

I laughed too soon. The next day, back home in Westchester, I picked up the phone and found a guy from the NCPA on the other end. "Something's come up," he said, clearly shaken. "You're going to be hearing from a reporter named Mike Lee from the *Fort Worth Star-Telegram*."

Not liking the sound of this, I didn't wait, but called the reporter first.

In retrospect, I'd have been better advised first to call a friend of mine, Stephen Michaud, a reporter at the *Star-Telegram* himself from 1994 to 1998. As he told me when I reached him afterward, in its approach to social issues, and especially race, the *Star-Telegram* is a model of heavy-handed P.C. "When the current executive editor came in, he sent around a memo saying we were all to heighten our P.C. awareness and diversity sensitivity. This was to be a line item in annual job reviews, and it was to extend even to the copy editors, though no one could explain how copy editors could increase a newspaper's coverage of diversity."

When I called him, Mike Lee got right to the point. They'd had reports that I'd made racially inflammatory statements, he said. What did I have to say about that?

I replied that it was absurd and explained in some detail exactly what the speech had been about.

Well, might I have inadvertently made offensive remarks?

Look, I told him, starting to get seriously upset but trying to hide it, it's not the first time I've given this speech. I know what I said. It's based on my book: Why don't you take a look at *that*?

But my heart was sinking further by the second. Clearly, the story was essentially pre-written. I was about to be accused of racism. To be smeared on this of all subjects! I've cared passionately about racial justice as long as I can remember – every bit as much today as when I was a teenage civil rights worker, picketing and singing "We Shall Overcome." Would it have been worth bothering to explain that to this guy? Or, indeed, that my ideological shift was brought on in part by my belated recognition that liberalism's feel-good, shopworn approaches to the race question, so reliant on the proposition that you can solve discrimination by discriminating against someone else, could only increase racial animosity?

No, none of that mattered. "This is disgraceful," I told him instead. "It's Kafkaesque, and I want you to quote me on that."

For just a moment I thought I might actually have gotten through. Well, he allowed, he was still trying to track down those who'd attended the session; he'd call to give me a chance to respond to any complaints before he wrote up the piece.

He didn't.

Early the following week, I heard from a friend who lives in Dallas. "What the hell did you say down here?"

Mike Lee's article, co-written with a staffer for the paper in Washington, was an exceedingly nasty piece of work, a catalogue of half-truths and insinuations, profoundly unfair, but also rather deft, in that none of that was readily apparent to the untrained eye. Starting on page one and running over 1,100 words, it began with a fundamental mischaracterization of what had occurred and took off from there: "Federal Reserve Bank directors from the Dallas and San Francisco districts were stunned when a conservative author's luncheon speech at the Dallas bank turned into a lecture about political correctness, blacks, gays, and women who put their children in day care."

Throughout, things I had said were taken out of context, stripped of tone, and otherwise misrepresented. Lee had been granted access to a video of the speech but was highly selective in what he used. On the key issue, the *Huck Finn* anecdote, the point I was making is nowhere to be found, but Jones's noble-sounding declaration – with its damning accusation about my "seemingly rationalizing of the word 'n——'" – is quoted in full. (In fact, that's the only reason I can reproduce it verbatim here.) Of course, my response goes unrecorded. What, then, had provoked Jones's outburst in the first place? "[Stein] also described an argument his son had with a teacher about Mark Twain's *The Adventures of Huckleberry Finn*, and repeated a racial slur that is in the book."

Jones evidently refused further comment for the article, but the reporters played big a statement they elicited from a spokesperson for his associate, Robert Parry, the head of the San Francisco Fed, to the effect that Parry had "found the speaker's choice of words to be offensive and inappropriate for a gathering held at a Federal Reserve bank." Needless to say, no one who actually liked the speech was quoted, but, in the sort of flimsy pretense to fairness such reporters describe as balance, the "conservative author" who'd "stunned" the gathering with his "offensive" and "inappropriate" remarks is allowed a single quotation in self-defense: "'When I was telling the *Huck Finn* story, he just heard the n-word,' Stein said. 'Ninety-five percent of the people in that room got it.'" But lacking the essential context that my point was the book's powerful *anti*-racist message, even the most astute reader surely wondered: Got what?

It is truly a sickening feeling being slandered in this way, the outrage mixing with a profound sense of helplessness. Yet rereading the article, I finally grasped something else: I was not really the main target here. Bob McTeer was.

A quick visit to the Internet showed why. Well-liked and well-respected, with a squeaky-clean reputation, he was a favorite of local conservatives, and had been described as "the leader of the free enterprise Fed." "Alone among FOMC members," noted Lawrence Kudlow in a March 2002 column, "McTeer uses real-time financial and commodity advice to guide his policy views. . . . [I]t remains unlikely that Alan Greenspan will serve out his full term as Fed chairman through 2004. To promote non-inflationary growth and monetary reform, why not Bob McTeer?"

And, sure enough, there it all was near the top of the *Star-Telegram* story: "Bob McTeer, president of the Federal Reserve Bank of Dallas, quickly apologized to his colleagues, but the flap has reached officials in Washington, D.C., where McTeer, popular for his folksy manner and steadfast belief in free markets, has been considered a possible successor to Fed chairman Alan Greenspan."

In fact, McTeer – whose photo illustrates the piece – is a very classy guy, and his apology-under-duress proved to be about as tepid as they come: "'I personally didn't think [the author] was out of line,' McTeer said, but added, 'I regret it and I'm sorry that it happened.'"

Over subsequent days, as other papers around the state not only picked up the story but cast it in ever uglier terms, each of them similarly featured McTeer as a principal. *The Dallas Morning News* story, appearing the following day, began: "In a speech on political correctness last week, conservative author Harry Stein made comments about affirmative action, blacks, gays, and feminism that offended some audience members, including several members of the Dallas and San Francisco Federal Reserve Banks. Of particular offense to some was Mr. Stein's use of a derogatory racial term for blacks." The article added that the speech "had also caught the attention of lawmakers in Washington" and quoted Representative Ken Bentsen (D-Houston), a member of the House Financial Services Committee, as observing that "the incident could have the potential of hurting Mr. McTeer in Senate confirmation hearings." In addition, there was the report in the *Austin American-Statesman*, which, after dutifully reporting that I had "repeated a racial slur," added, "In Washington, a spokesman for the Federal Reserve declined to say whether McTeer faced disciplinary action as a result of the speech, which shocked people in the audience."

Hardly incidentally, the beleaguered McTeer now came forth with a new and stronger statement, saying, "Certain derogatory terms for racial and religious minorities are so inflammatory and offensive that they have no place in a serious policy discussion. Our speaker's use of these words deeply offended many present."

Given the pressure McTeer was under, I understood and even sympathized. But of course the damage was done. Should he ever be nominated for higher office, there is now a potentially fatal land mine buried in his record.

Watching it all from afar, emotionally involved yet physically detached, I was struck most by the alacrity with which so many who might have done the right thing ducked for cover. Particularly notable for its inaction was the NCPA, an independent organization, unlike the Fed, and ostensibly libertarian. Though I did get a couple of emails from members of the group who'd been present, remarking on the irony of a speech decrying political correctness itself being subject to the most heavy-handed P.C. – one rightly referred to McTeer as having been "Borked" – the group's leaders were silent, failing to stand up and publicly decry the false accusations of racism against its invited speaker.

It didn't take long for things to settle down. After a few days, there was no further mention of the episode in the papers. Though I was told that staffers for the racially opportunistic Maxine Waters, who sits on the House Committee on Financial Services, which oversees the Fed, were calling around about the episode, barring the sixty-one-year-old McTeer's nomination to a top post, it would likely not surface publicly again.

Why then bring it up now? I do not, believe me, have a martyr complex; for a while there, the mere mention of the city of Dallas – even of the Texas Rangers baseball team – made my heart skip a beat.

Still, the mere fact that this calumny was out there, on the record, permanently available on the web, made my blood boil. My wife and kids were incensed. Reluctant as I was to get into it all again, the thought that this slur would be allowed to win the day kept me from just walking away. When my editor at *City Journal*, the publication of the Manhattan Institute, suggested a piece on the subject, I dove back in.

Working the phone to report the article only strengthened my resolve. William Jones of San Francisco, the man whose remarks after my speech started it all, never returned my calls. I did reach Mike Lee, the reporter for the *Star-Telegram*, who picked up his own phone. In the fifteen or so minutes we talked, there were many silences from his end, repeated suggestions that I take the matter up with his editor, and a slew of non-answers. Why hadn't he called back as he said he would? "I thought I did. It's been a while." You saw a video of the speech: Was there anything even remotely racist about it? "I don't think we called you a racist." But you very strongly implied I was, didn't you? That was certainly the impression everyone seemed to get. A very long silence. "I think you should talk to Lois," he said for the fourth time.

I did. Lois Norder, the *Star-Telegram*'s northeast editor, embodied every one of the attitudes – the smug self-assurance, the presumption to superior virtue, the pose (in the face of an avalanche of evidence to the contrary) of objectivity – that makes so many despise today's mainstream press. Her position was that since the paper had never explicitly called me a racist (or, at any rate, hadn't used the actual word), my complaints about the piece's objectivity were unfounded. When I asked Norder whether she herself thought *Huck Finn* was a racist book, her frigid, expressionless voice got even flatter. "The story is well-sourced," she said dismissively. "The story is fair."

"Fair! Doesn't the truth of what happened even matter? You guys wanted to stir up a controversy when there wasn't anything there – and that's what you did!" She didn't miss a beat. "As a journalist, you should understand that someone involved in something does not have an unbiased view. You're seeing it through your filter. Our job is not to see it through any filter."

So there it was. Not only was I, at the very least, racially insensitive; I wasn't even a serious person. And what was most unsettling, finally, is that the woman probably wasn't even being cynical. Given her conception of her role as a journalist, she probably didn't experience a flicker of self-doubt or bad conscience; after all, the P.C. filter through which she and so many other journalists see the world not only presumes that every accusation of bigotry is valid but that anyone who doesn't toe the liberal line is fair game.

Weeks after my speech, someone who was present for my talk wrote me a supportive letter. Given the shameful denouement of the whole episode, he observed, "It is a miracle the story didn't end up on page one above the fold in *The New York Times*."

But here's the good part. When the piece appeared, I got a tidal wave of support, literally hundreds of letters and emails; a fair number of these from the Dallas area, including quite a few from *Star-Telegram* readers announcing they'd cancelled their subscriptions. A couple mentioned they'd contacted the offending reporter and editor personally for an old-fashioned, Texas-style dressing down.

So, yes, I was very, very glad I went public.

That's the thing about reporters – and, indeed, about so many blue-state liberals in general: They're used to operating unchallenged, surrounded by their own kind. Fight back, and invariably they begin to crumble. There's a word for people like this. Bullies.

Social Work: The Scum of All Professions

ENOUGH SAID

HERE'S A TINY BIT of solace for fellow conservatives stuck in fields, like journalism, where the closest thing to an ideological ally is likely to be the radio secretly tuned to Rush: It could always be worse.

Try this for an oxymoron: *conservative social worker.*

It's an open question whether such a being even exists. We might as well jet off to Mauritius for a stab at unearthing the long-extinct dodo. In fact, the rules governing the profession actually forbid anyone who rejects the leftist line to so much as enter the field. Really. It's right there in the Code of Ethics of the Council on Social Work Education, the exclusive accreditor of schools of social work, that "social work education programs [must] integrate social and economic justice content grounded in an understanding of distributive justice, human and civil rights, and the global interconnections of oppression."

The closest I could come up with to the real thing was a *former* social work student named Bill Felkner who tried, and failed, to buck the system. Felkner's travails from 2004 to 2006 as an MSW candidate at the (publicly funded) College of Rhode Island make for a long and harrowing story. The gist of it is that when he objected to the hard-left indoctrination that passed for instruction in his classes – he found mandatory viewing of Michael Moore's *Fahrenheit 9/11* especially irksome – he was slapped down like the reactionary wretch he'd shown himself to be.

One professor sharply reminded him, in writing, that "as a profession we do take sides," and that social work is a "value-based profession that clearly articulates a socio-political ideology about how the world works and how the world should be." Lest there remain any doubt, the professor added, "I revel in my biases. So, I think that anyone who consistently holds antithetical views to those that are espoused by the profession might ask themselves whether social work is the profession for them." Another professor readily seconded this, noting, "We hope that all social workers are liberal." Informed that his failure to fall in line meant he would "not be able to meet the academic requirements necessary to obtain a degree," the noble Felkner finally threw in the towel and quit the field.

I should note that there might be another social work insurrectionist lurking out there somewhere. When I googled "conservative social worker," up popped this curious dispatch, unsigned:

Whats so wrong about being a conservative social worker?

I'm in social work and am supposed to be practicing under a liberal stand point, but i often find myself questioning my beliefs when i do things that doesn't seem right. for example, there are some desires i have like going to shop for brand name clothing, but at the same time i feel bad when i think about my goal as a profession. one of my professors as another example refuses to shop at walmart because she has this imbedded idea that it's the scum of all stores. so I'm having a hard time trying to understand why so many students like myself i guess say they take policy and helping people out who are homeless or those that don't have guidance in life so seriously, but at the same time we lavish ourselves with the expensive things in life? are we just being hypocrites or are we all in nature just conservatives at heart? are social workers just screwed in the head and are all emotionally disturbed? I'm not really sure if social work is really for me anymore. . .

Admittedly, this could well be a forgery, and a clumsy one at that, created by actual social workers to libel any counter-revolutionaries in their midst as semi-literate. But the last few (extremely insightful) lines cast doubt on that theory. If this is indeed real, the author is urged to contact me forthwith, care of this book's publisher.

Right in the Land of the Tenured Leftist

A JOB DIRTIER THAN
ROADKILL COLLECTOR

AMONG CONSERVATIVES, it is all-too-common knowledge, but let's put it in terms the average liberal might begin to grasp: What acid rain is to our irreplaceable forests, lakes, and streams, leftist dogma is to American higher education. In every corner of the land, it has turned once-flourishing departments of English and history into barren wastelands where only the academic equivalent of cockroaches can thrive. Its corrosive poison – infantile anti-Americanism, hatred of capitalism, scorn for ideological pluralism – spreads far beyond the narrow confines of its source, polluting popular culture, public education, the very laws under which we live. Absorbed in sufficiently high doses, it is morally and intellectually fatal.

No, probably not even that explanation would do the trick. While the mind-boggling damage done to higher education by multicultural activists, diversity-mongers, and all-around leftist jerks is a subject very much on the minds of conservatives, liberals seem truly not to care. More precisely, they actually regard it as progress. Shakespeare elbowed aside by Maya Angelou? Hey, education's got to change with the times, just like the Constitution. Mandatory sensitivity training for incoming freshmen to instill appreciation of transgendered persons? What kind of monster has a problem with sensitivity? Conservative students getting charged with hate speech for daring to take on affirmative action or women's studies zealots? Exactly – *that* kind of monster.

Even the occasional report in the mainstream press of epidemic ideological conformity on the nation's campuses fails to elicit a reaction. So what if, as the *Washington Post* reports, 80 percent of faculty in America's English literature, philosophy, and political science departments describe themselves as liberal and a mere 5 percent as conservative – with ratios of eighteen to one at Brown, twenty-six to one at Cornell, and sixteen to one at UCLA – or that a study after the 2004 election showed that the Harvard faculty gave John Kerry thirty-one dollars for every dollar donated to George Bush, with the ratios rising to forty-three to one at MIT and three hundred to one at Princeton? (And you think when someone gets around to a comprehensive analysis of the 2008 campaign donations, that will be any *less* lopsided?) For liberals, the only important question remains what it's always been: How can I get my kid into one of those places?

Nor, of course, have such revelations made the slightest dent where it matters most, on the campus itself. Rosemary G. Feal, former executive director of the Modern Language Association – which makes or breaks the reputations of those who teach English and other languages at the university level, or hope to – reacted to one such survey with the huffy indignation of Margaret Dumont: "It boggles my mind the degree to which this is rubbish."

This brings us to those at the short end of those ridiculous ratios: conservative academics, who've actually forged careers on the modern campus, or tried to.

Frankly, it beats me why anyone would opt for this world of punishment. Better to go for one of those positions featured on "Dirty Jobs," like roadkill collector or mosquito control officer, or one of those guys who fashions garden pots out of cow manure.

But they seem to have their reasons. Take my friend Garry Apgar, whom I met in the late Seventies, while working on an English-language newspaper in Paris. Garry was a Vietnam vet studying art history at the Sorbonne under the G.I. Bill. But he was also a terrific illustrator – I still have a wonderful ersatz *Guernica* he did, with French politicians of the era in place of Picasso's horse, bull, and tortured human figures – so was working for the paper as a cartoonist. Along the way, he also contributed a couple of pieces on Voltaire, in whom he had a passionate interest; even now, he is president of the Voltaire Society, and lectures often on the man and his work.

But his goal in life was to teach art history at the college level, and in 1980 he returned to the States to pursue it. He went to Yale, got his Ph.D., became Dr. Apgar. Things seemed to be going splendidly.

Yet somehow his academic career never panned out. He never landed a full-time academic post. Eventually, the financial stress threatened his marriage, and he ended up teaching high school French.

What happened? A few things – but very high on the list is the fact that, though the opposite of combative, Garry is a conservative, and makes no attempt to hide the fact.

"I was always a conservative – *ab ovo*, from the egg," Garry says, "and at first I really didn't think it would be a problem." Indeed, his dissertation, on a little-known eighteenth-century Swiss artist named Jean Hubert – he'd been drawn to the subject by his interest in Hubert's neighbor and most frequent subject, Voltaire – won him a coveted Kress Fellowship; it was subsequently published, in French, in a handsome and amply illustrated edition. Garry received particular notice for his original research on the project, unearthing long-forgotten letters and other archival material, drawing hitherto unknown connections between people, "all the stuff that's now pooh poohed by cutting-edge scholars concerned with deconstructionism and all that."

In brief, he appeared well launched. Out of Yale, he got a job teaching at a small northeastern college. (He asks I not use the name because he's "still got friends there, and it's not a great school; if you had a pulse and money to pay, you got in.") After a year, he was up for an open tenure-track position. But then . . . the job was offered to someone else, a woman less credentialed and clearly less qualified.

It turned out that he'd had the misfortune of breaking into the field just as things were turning dramatically worse for people of the wrong gender (male), hue (white), and sexual orientation (what, until a few years earlier, would have almost everywhere have been categorized as "normal").

For his part, all Garry knew was that what had happened was not remotely fair. So, after thinking it over, he did the unthinkable: He complained. All these years later, he can only shake his head at his naïveté. "The corruption argument never gets you anywhere. Either they're so ideological they genuinely don't see it, or they're so cynical they don't care. It's like thinking you're going to embarrass Claude Raines in *Casablanca*. People like that are essentially amoral, Clinton types – and they're everywhere in academia."

Not that he hadn't been warned. His old advisor from Yale, herself a committed feminist, "yelled at me on the phone. 'Don't contest this,' she said. 'If you know what's good for you, you'll just withdraw and walk away.' I mean, there was this implied mafioso threat. But she was right. I got a reputation as a troublemaker."

He pauses. "The fact is, if I'd been a woman and lodged such an accusation, it would've scared them to death. Even if I'd been totally wrong, they'd have either given me the job or a fat settlement. But as a white male, and a known conservative, I was dead." Nor, obviously, was he helped by his choice of specialty, eighteenth-century European art. "It's not exactly trendy. There's not much room there to get in gay theory." He laughs. "Though I suppose there are those who would try."

After that, there were a string of one-year visiting professorships – at the University of Delaware, Brown, and Princeton, plus a year in Lyon, teaching in French – but never another tenure-track job. "I kept applying," he says, "but I kept getting aced out by a woman or a minority. The system is medieval, a culture of powerful, interwoven alliances – gays and lesbians and straight Marxists and feminists – and they do the recruiting and hiring. They'll find a zillion excuses to obscure the real reasons: 'the scholarship's a little flimsy,' 'it's not a good fit,' or whatever they want. There's no alliance of straight conservatives, or even old-fashioned, open-minded liberals."

Along the way, he saw fools and incompetents getting ahead by the boatload, and cronyism that would have embarrassed Boss Tweed's Tammany Hall, as well as more fear than he saw as a Marine back in Vietnam. "In my field, in particular, there was open contempt for straight people – they'd be off handedly referred to as 'breeders.' This is the milieu you're in as a conservative – or just as a reasonable person. It was like being in the old Soviet Union. You had to be constantly vigilant about what you said and to whom you said it. The only way to express yourself honestly was by samizdat."

So why did he put himself through it for so long? "What can I tell you?" he offers rather sheepishly. "I love teaching, even if doing it means climbing into a playpen full of angry, infantile narcissists."

What he doesn't say, because he's not a self-aggrandizing kind of guy, is that what he was doing was damned *important*. A few generations hence, Jean Hubert will likely be all but lost to history – quite possibly soon to be followed by his buddy Voltaire. The dwindling band of conservatives on the nation's campuses are doing nothing less than fighting to preserve the Western intellectual tradition.

The Cold War historian Ron Radosh started on the opposite end of the political spectrum from Garry, but he too was done in, and far more publicly, by what, on the modern campus, is that most dangerous of traits: intellectual honesty. Having come of age on the left, he was persuaded by extensive research that iconic victim Julius Rosenberg was in fact guilty of the espionage for which he'd been executed, and said as much in a 1983 book, *The Rosenberg File*, that he co-authored. He expected a vigorous dialogue on the subject; instead, he found himself almost universally condemned by his colleagues for daring to write such a thing at all.

"They'd have nothing to do with me," he says. "I wasn't an honest researcher. I was a traitor to the cause. I was at a conference not long afterward and Paul Buell, a leftist historian I'd known for years, walked away when I went to say hello. Later that night, I saw him in the empty lobby, and he said, 'Now I can say hello to you, because nobody's watching. But, seriously, you *are* a running dog of imperialism.'" Radosh laughs. "There was this other woman from Hofstra, Carolyn Eisenberg, who came up to me and said, 'I just want you to know you used to be one of our heroes and models, but you've betrayed us all; what you did was horrible.' At that, she started crying."

To these and innumerable others in his field, Radosh has remained a pariah ever since: "It never ends. They don't forget. As a result of that, I was blackballed, could never get any other really good job." He cites one episode as especially telling, an interview with the entire history faculty at George Washington University. "They didn't even bother to pretend. There was no discussion of my credentials as an historian, or my writing, just my politics. It was: 'Why are you right-wing?' and 'Why do you write these books saying these victims of McCarthyism were guilty?' Around the table they went, one after another condemning me for my politics. I ended up getting two votes from the whole department."

Moreover, says Radosh, surveying the academic scene, he sees no prospect of things getting better any time soon. "I was looking recently at the annual catalogue of the Organization of American Historians, the branch that specializes in U.S. history, and it was like reading the names of the Communist Party annual conference. One hundred percent left-wing and anti-American. Every paper was about class and gender and the oppression of women by the patriarchy."

Stephen H. Balch, president emeritus of the National Association of Scholars, a group of conservatives in academia who came together in the Eighties to fight the scourge of political correctness on the nation's campuses, confirms that assessment. "We imagined," he writes of the group's founding, "that the grown-ups on campus only needed to be reminded of their responsibilities to put things right. After all, how could serious scholars permit higher education to descend into speech codes, racial quotas, and political indoctrination? Or preside over the trashing of the core curriculum, Western civilization, and the American founding?

"Boy, were we naïve! Today we have Ward Churchill, Sami Al-Arian, the Duke 88, as well as entirely 'postmodernized' academic programs and university requirements, devoted to ensuring that students, who may know little else, know loads about diversity, feminism, global warming, the failures of capitalism, and the hypocrisy of Thomas Jefferson."

So the horror stories keep on coming, only now the protagonists are a new generation of conservatives. "I really never believed it could be this bad," admits a young conservative historian named Mark Moyar, on the job market for five years and still looking. A summa cum laude graduate of Harvard, with a doctorate from Cambridge and a highly regarded book to his credit, at this writing he has been turned down for nearly two hundred tenure-track jobs. "I mean, I figured there'd at least be jobs for the token conservative, so that if I worked hard and did a really exceptional job, I'd slip in. At this point, it's just bizarre – especially seeing the caliber of people who *are* getting hired. In place after place, the Baby Boomers in senior positions demand total and absolute ideological conformity and, if anything, the younger scholars who came up under their tutelage are even worse."

It is surely a vast understatement to say that Moyar's book hasn't exactly helped. Entitled *Triumph Forsaken*, it argues that the Vietnam war was not only winnable, but should have been won. Then again, who knows? I spoke to another young conservative academic, an English Ph.D., who's taken the opposite tack, try-ing hard to avoid politics in her life as an academic, and mostly succeeding. Still, she's the opposite of a shrinking violet and knows her *private* conservative views have hurt her.

"I was an immigrant from Slovenia who struggled to get herself into graduate school," she puts it to me in an email, "and when I did I encountered professors who hated literature. These were people who disparaged all the beauty that as a girl I found through my library card. One, who taught a T. S. Eliot seminar, so despised Eliot for the sins of 'racism' and 'misogyny' that he'd sometimes get so exercised he would literally start foaming at the mouth; he now is co-chair of the English department at a publicly-funded university." Alas, she briefly tangled with this guy en route to her doctorate, and has "not been able to obtain a tenure-track posi-tion, nor even to get a paper accepted at the MLA convention." She now has a temporary post at a community college, where she "will be making about $12,000 this semester (no benefits), teach-ing five classes."

How do the tenured radicals who run liberal arts departments justify this state of affairs? "We try to hire the best, smartest people available," explains Robert Brandon, the chairman of Duke's phi-losophy department. "If, as John Stuart Mill said, stupid people are generally conservative, then there are lots of conservatives we will never hire."

Can this sinking ship be turned around? Probably the most reckless bookie wouldn't take that bet. Still, if anything's worth that old college try. . .

Recent years have seen at least one encouraging development: the success of the James Madison Program in American Ideals at Princeton. Created in 2000, under the direction of Robert George, the school's McCormick Professor of Jurisprudence (and presumably the one in that three hundred to one ratio), the Madi-son Program focuses on American constitutional law and Western political tradition. As Stanley Kurtz observes, with the University of Chicago having lately dropped the ball, "Princeton is rapidly becoming the key quality alternative for producing a new genera-tion of conservative intellectuals."

What's key is that George raises independent funding for the program, insulating it from the pressures that the well-organized campus left would surely otherwise bring to bear to undermine it. In this sense and others, Madison has been a model for conserva-tives at other institutions seeking to establish similar free-thought zones. To date, no fewer than ten such oases of intellectual plural-ism are either going concerns or in the works, at such schools as Brown, Georgetown, NYU, Boston College, and the University of Colorado; the conservative Manhattan Institute, through its Veri-tas Fund, has given $2,500,000 to help them along.

Then again, there's the case of Hamilton College, in upstate Clinton, New York. Here, too, three professors were well on their way to creating such an enterprise. It was to be called the Alexan-der Hamilton Center, aimed at promoting "excellence in scholar-ship through the study of freedom, democracy, and capitalism as these ideas were developed and institutionalized in the United States and within the larger tradition of Western culture." All seemed to be going along splendidly. After a siege of terrible leftist-generated publicity – the school's Kirkland Project for the Study of Gender, Society & Culture first invited the convicted terrorist Susan Rosenberg to teach at Hamilton, then invited the notorious plagiarist and terrorist-sympathizer Ward Churchill to give a lec-ture – the academically rigorous AHC seemed like an opportu-nity to reassert the school's seriousness of purpose. By the fall of 2006, its sponsors had raised a ton of cash, including $3.6 million from a single prominent alum, and had the administration fully on board. A press release issued by the school characterized the AHC as "an exciting faculty initiative."

Then it all came apart. At a faculty meeting, there was pre-sented a resolution, pushed by members of the Kirkland Project, demanding Hamilton exercise institutional control over the

AHC's policies and programs – i.e., strip it of the very independence that was its *raison d'être*. The resolution passed 77 to 17. "Frankly," says Robert Paquette, the American history professor who was the AHC's most public proponent and slated to serve as its executive director, "I was surprised we got seventeen."

What was ultimately fatal to the center's prospects was the fact that key members of the Board of Trustees soon also came down on the AHC, demanding ultimate supervisory control. Though Paquette and his colleagues were prepared to make numerous changes in their initial proposal, this was a bridge way too far. The college soon disavowed the project.

The ensuing months were highly acrimonious, with the college seeking to shift blame for its own cowardliness. "Having then reneged on the deal," Paquette says, "they proceeded to tell serial lies to the public."

Absolutely fearless, Paquette is a source of immense discomfort to his adversaries. "I know there are important people around here who want to get rid of me in the worst way," he says, matter-of-factly, adding he is the "only out-of-closet conservative on a faculty of two hundred." How many secret ones are there? "Less than five."

But Paquette's not going anywhere. "This fight's too important – it's for the future, it's for our posterity, it's for our country. This is a great civilization, and we're at risk."

If there was not an altogether happy ending to the AHC saga, he and his colleagues have at least forged a reasonable facsimile. In 2007, they opened the newly rechristened Alexander Hamilton *Institute* (after the school attempted to copyright the original name behind their back) as a privately-run enterprise, based in a mansion about a mile from campus. Having lost the funding that comes with a relationship with the school, the AHC's budget is tiny and almost all work is done by volunteers. But its inaugural year far exceeded expectations; its scholarly meetings and events attract a wide range of locals (including many home schoolers), as well as members of the Hamilton community. Four conservative and libertarian student groups from Hamilton meet there regularly to hash out politics, public policy, and cultural history, and, says Paquette, they remark often on "how refreshing it is to come to a place where they can speak comfortably about complex issues." He pauses. "'Speak comfortably,' those are the words you keep hearing. It says something, doesn't it, when you've got students paying fifty thousand dollars a year to come to Hamilton College, and they have to leave campus to have that kind of free and open conversation?"

Looking for Love in All the Wrong Places

WE'RE TALKING ENTIRE
ZIP CODES, CONGRESSIONAL
DISTRICTS, STATES, REGIONS

ON OCTOBER 10, 2007, Page Six, the *New York Post*'s renowned gossip section, ran an item entitled "Oddest Couple of the Decade: Lifelong Democrat Andrew Stein and arch-conservative cutie Ann Coulter." It read, in full: "The former city council president (when there was such a title) first took Coulter – author of *If Democrats Had Any Brains, They'd Be Republicans* – to the black-tie Lincoln Center Film Society gala two weeks ago, where they turned heads. More recently, they were at Soho House 'in passionate liplock,' according to a witness. Stein told Page Six: 'She's attacked a lot of my friends, but what can I say, opposites attract!' So do blondes with ultra-long legs."

Inquiring minds obviously needed to know more, so on October 25, there appeared a follow-up: "While the leggy blonde was dining with Andrew Stein at Centolire on Madison Avenue the other night, a wild-eyed man came up to their table and shouted at Coulter for her right-wing views and at Stein for dating her. Stein told the heckler, 'Listen pal, get lost and learn some manners!'"

When Andrew Stein was first getting started in politics, I spent some time covering him, and liked the guy's brash self-confidence, so, crazy romantic that I am, I was delighted to see he was still his own man and ready to do battle with frothing liberal weenies in defense of the lovely Ann.

But, as with Romeo and Juliet or Ellen DeGeneres and Anne Heche, it wasn't fated to be.

The inevitable denouement came in early January 2008. Quoth Page Six: "They said the unholy union between wacky conservative TV pundit/author Ann Coulter and former City Council president and Democrat Andrew Stein, which was first reported on this page, wouldn't work – and they were right. It's over. When reached for comment, Stein would only say, 'we split because of irreconcilable differences.' The two dated for 2½ (very long) months."

In retrospect, what's startling is that a prominent Democrat, even one long gone from the political arena, could have believed for ten minutes that he could get away with such an association without paying a steep price. Where has he been all these years? Love may be blind, but no one claims it also turns one deaf, dumb, or unable to read *The New York Times* in Braille. Where he presumably saw Ann as an incredibly interesting woman, good-looking, full of wicked humor, and generally a lot of fun to be with – and, yes, in her professional life, a sharp, caustic, often over-the-top book-selling machine – to lots of liberals, she is a cross between Eva Braun and her boyfriend – minus their good points!

In the realm of romance, as in every other, there is a fundamental difference in the way those on opposite sides regard one another: Conservatives think liberals have bad ideas, while liberals think conservatives are evil.

Bruce Tinsley, who draws the conservative comic strip "Mallard Fillmore," and is married to a liberal civil rights lawyer, has all kinds of firsthand exposure to this phenomenon. "All her liberal friends are incredulous that our marriage works," he observes, "but none of my conservative friends have any trouble with it at all. They understand you can think differently about things and still be civil to one another."

It's tough to feel sorry for Ann Coulter, but, romance-wise, she's in the same boat as lots of other conservatives in Blue America –

and it's not the one captained by Gavin MacLeod. "When a woman learns I'm a conservative," says Bernard Chapin, a thirty-eight-year-old school psychologist from Chicago, "the first reaction is usually shock or disbelief. After all, I don't *look* like their idea of a conservative. I don't dress in pinstriped suits or green golf pants or" – he laughs – "have fangs. The second reaction is usually some version of 'see you later.'"

In an amusing piece he wrote on the web about his travails on the dating front, he notes that, though he's passionate about his politics, face to face with a potential love interest, he tries his damndest to keep them under wraps. Alas, inevitably, in one way or another, they always surface. He writes of dodging one woman's insistent question about when he planned to see Michael Moore's *Fahrenheit 9/11* until he could take it no more, and finally burst out, "Fuck that fat bastard!" In another example, a woman he was interested in was coming to his home for the first time on short notice. After frantically cleaning the bathroom and otherwise dousing the place in Clorox, he thought he was in good shape, until he found the woman staring at the portrait of George W. Bush he'd been sent by the RNC.

"What is this?" she spat.

He confesses that "a man of true principle" would have not only "pointed out George's merits, but that some things are more important than winning political debates." Instead he opted to wimp out. "I have no idea," he told her. "I don't know who that person is. I wonder why he's hanging on my wall."

That won him the hoped-for smile, but the reprieve was only temporary. A little while later, in the bathroom, he says, "She stumbled across my Hillary Clinton doormat." This time the pleading ignorance bit fell flat, and afterward he engaged in some post-game self-recrimination. He realized that in response to her shocked "What's this doing here?" he should have replied with the more suitably Clintonian "I cannot recall."

I have one conservative friend, a recently divorced middle-

aged guy living in the college town of Middlebury, Connecticut –
where, as he puts it, "If you supported Joe Lieberman, a lot of
people around here think you're a total reactionary" – who does
most of his dating via the web-site Match.com. But here, too, his
beliefs have done him the opposite of good. "It's a nightmare.
There've been several women who immediately stopped writing
after I admitted I vote Republican. There was another with whom
I thought things were going well enough that I risked sending her
something by one of my favorite conservative writers, Victor
Davis Hanson. She wrote back with the most irrational screed
you've ever seen. She didn't comment on the piece at all, just
wrote that she seemed to recall reading in a review in *The New
York Times Book Review* that Hanson was a bad writer, which, as far
as she was concerned, settled the issue. Oh, yes, she also noticed
he was identified as working at the Hoover Institute and writing
for *National Review*. Even more proof that he (and I) were worthless dirtbags! That was the end of that."

By now, my friend is almost ready to give up the whole business. He notes that, while there exist dating websites geared for
conservatives and/or Republicans, in his area the pickings are so
pitifully thin as to approach nonexistence. Rather than continue
to waste everyone's time, he's considering opening his own profile
on Match.com with the following: "Dear Confused, Bleeding-
Heart, Race-Hustling, America-Hating Feminist. I am a knuckle-
dragging armchair warmonger looking for love. Can we talk?"

But even he concedes that younger conservatives, like those at
nearby Wesleyan University, probably have it tougher. After all,
as a reformed radical Sixties veteran, he fondly recalls the considerable social benefits that come with having the right (which is to
say, left) politics in college and on into early adulthood.

People on the right like to talk about the burgeoning number
of College Republican clubs on the nation's campuses, making the
point that in the prevailing climate of oppressive political correctness, it is free-thinking individualists on the right who are today's

rebels against the status quo. And of course this is so. But let's be frank here. During the 2008 presidential campaign, how many young couples came together, if often only for a few hours, at Barack Obama rallies? How many met at events for John McCain, or Fred Thompson, or Rudy Giuliani?

A story in the *New York Daily News* in advance of a September 2007 Obama rally in downtown Manhattan got right to the heart of the matter:

It'll be a raging pickup scene. The rally from 5–8 P.M. in Washington Square Park promises to draw a young, intelligent crowd. And what better time to hook up than a beautiful fall evening while waving a banner for democracy?

"You are likely to have similar political views, and those often cross into other things that aren't politically affiliated," says Colleen Kluttz, a 29-year-old TV producer who's hitting the event tonight if work allows. "It will give you something to talk about. It gives you a reason to have conversations that aren't just about yourself." But what kind of guy are you going to find at an Obama rally?

"A socially conscious liberal – probably a well-dressed, well-groomed hipster," Kluttz says.

But when the sun goes down over NYU, the party really starts about 20 blocks north – the rally after-party.

The Obama campaign is in no way affiliated with the Official Barack in NYC After-party, set for 7:30 at the 40/40 Club in the Flatiron District, but you can bet the young and the restless will file up Fifth Ave. from the park to continue, well, showing their support. Even the invite for the event reads like a singles bash: "Hope hits the Big Apple! Join us at Jay-Z's 40/40 Club on Thursday as we ride the winds of change from the hottest rally in New York. Move to the music, socialize with friends, and let your voice be heard as we celebrate with audacity.

Lindsay Schaeffer, 25, may even skip the rally for the nighttime bash.

"Look, you never meet good guys in a bar," she reasons. "Something like this naturally weeds out the losers for you. You aren't going to get some pickup artist at a political after-party."

One ardent Obama supporter (who declined to give his name because he works in politics) says he'll attend both the rally and the after-party, and he doesn't expect to be going home alone. He's confident for a reason. "Let's face it: Leftie girls are easy," he says.

From the perspective of the lonely young conservative looking for love, once Obama clinched the nomination, things got even worse. One pro-Obama website, the memorably-named Blue Balled, produced a hugely popular Internet short that had a guy picking up a drop-dead gorgeous woman at a singles bar and taking her back to his place. Things are moving along nicely until, searching for a condom in his bedside table, she spots a photo of John McCain. "I only sleep with Democrats!" she erupts, leaving him, as it were, high and dry.

Not, of course, that this is anything new. My friend Sol Stern recalls how, even back in the relatively staid Fifties, "kids on the left had it pretty easy in that respect. At CCNY, where I went, that was always a great recruiting tool for the Labor Youth League – 'girls put out.' They were 'liberated' even before feminism."

A decade and a half later, when feminism was indeed the rage, young liberal men beyond number quickly grasped that the quickest way to get in good with women was by earnestly mouthing some of the movement's choicer platitudes. I know – I was one of them. Like many others, I especially stressed the fiction that, since the sexes are not merely equal but share identical biological impulses, politically advanced women should be as sexually indiscriminate as we men were.

One of my first pieces ever, appearing in 1973 in the long-defunct, self-consciously hip *New Times Magazine*, was an informal survey of the attitudes of such progressive young men on the feminist revolution. Among those I quoted was my aforementioned journalism school pal, Cary. Knowing all the right buttons to push, Cary was effusive in his praise of women's newfound assertiveness. "For years," he said, "I'd sit by the phone and wait for some beautiful girl to call. These days there's a chance that one might actually do it. This is why the liberated woman doesn't bother me at all. If someone else wants to take charge of the relationship, that's fine with me." A day after the piece appeared, a woman actually did track Cary down in his St. Louis home – as it turned out, not quite *beautiful*, but, hey! – and she immediately flew halfway across the country to spend the weekend with him.

Today Cary's son, Sam, is exactly the same age he was then – but conservative, which, since he lives and works in New York, means running the romantic race with lead weights around the ankles. "I just take it for granted that every girl I meet is going to be incredibly liberal," he says breezily, "so I'm very discreet. If a girl does find out what my politics are, I'll usually try to lessen the impact, by saying something like: 'But I'm not dogmatic about it; I also read *The New Yorker*.'" He laughs. "I mean, it's not a total lie. I do occasionally read something from *The New Yorker* on realclearpolitics.com."

"I read so much political stuff, left and right, that I have no trouble at all faking being a liberal," agrees his conservative buddy Pete Ambrosio. "I like to screw with people anyway, so on Facebook, I put up a picture of Obama instead of myself, along with a quote of his on abortion, where he said the left is too dogmatic about it." He pauses. "But I'm with Sam, I never bring up politics with girls. What's the point? One girl I dated actually created a group on Facebook that was called 'George Bush is Worse Than Osama Bin Laden.'"

"On the other hand," adds Sam, "at least in theory, the Internet is the best way for people like us to connect with women. I'm thinking maybe I'll start up a Facebook group honoring Bill Buckley and see how many decent-looking girls sign up."

Indeed, in bastions of "blue" thought, conservatives are left to find one another as best they can. A few years back, a couple right-of-center organizations at Harvard threw what they called a "Conservative Coming Out Dinner." Reading reports on the event, which drew a not exactly Obamaesque "several dozen undergraduates," one can't help be touched by the young conservatives' pluck. The Pledge of Allegiance was recited, presumably an alien sound in those environs, followed by an all-American menu of steak, potatoes, and pie, and, as after-dinner entertainment, "conservatives rose one at a time to tell anecdotes relating their experiences as members of what is perhaps Harvard's most misunderstood minority group." Somehow, admiration notwithstanding, it's hard not to think of the title of Nora Ephron's first book: *Wallflower at the Orgy*.

For conservatives, there is the comforting thought that, while romantic prospects might be in somewhat short supply, they at least know what they're looking for, values-wise – which is to say, the relationships they do forge are more likely than most to be grounded in trust and a shared worldview. There is a lot to be said for this, especially for women.

"Most of my conservative guy friends are comfortable dating liberal women," observes Bernadette Malone, a former editor with Penguin's conservative Sentinel imprint, who was fortunate enough to meet and marry a guy outside her own left-leaning industry who shares her politics, "but none of my conservative female friends will date liberal men."

The reason is obvious, at least to anyone who doesn't buy into the feminists' protracted war on nature: Conservative men tend to be men before they are conservative. (Among other things, this strikes me as the most plausible explanation for all the smart, conservative guys my age married to, and too often under the thumbs of, women with Gloria Steinem's politics. Most of them got married when their wives, like Steinhem herself, were in miniskirts.)

Then, too, women with serious conservative politics have invariably come to them the hard way, bucking their peers and the expectations of popular culture, and so often are especially impatient with "NPR men," as my wife terms that deeply annoying brand of smug, unnaturally soft-voiced, aggressively nonthreatening liberal male.

Such commitment to high principle – or, if you prefer, basic self respect – is a distinguishing characteristic of conservative women, young and old. As the Republican Club is probably the last place on any campus scouts for *Girls Gone Wild* head when on the prowl for recruits, so conservative women of my acquaintance in their thirties and forties regard too-adamant liberalism in a man as the ultimate deal breaker. "It's really pretty simple," observes Lindsay Young Craig, Vice President of Communications and Marketing at the Manhattan Institute, who married a fellow staffer. "Someone who shares your views on who should be president or the importance of individual rights will also share your beliefs on to how to raise children and the kinds of things they should be taught in school." Hers is, she notes, only one of a fair number of what she calls "think tank marriages."

None of this is to suggest there aren't also plenty of liberals out there with exemplary values – who treat their spouses with kindness and respect, put their children ahead of themselves, and in general comport themselves in a decent and responsible manner.

The difference is, they all loved Bill Clinton, who does none of those things.

Many, many, *many New York Times* features are at once staggeringly shallow and smugly certain, but none was more sure to provoke an instant spike in conservatives' blood pressure than one that appeared on February 17, 2008. Entitled "I Married a Republican: There, I Said It," it is by one Ann Hood. Calling herself "not just an average Democrat – I lean way, way left," she writes of her shame and embarrassment at finding herself partnered with a guy who seems, on the evidence, to be the most milquetoast moderate Republican imaginable. Nonetheless, Hood tells how friends and family recoiled when her "dirty secret" was revealed. "Clinton was president then, popular and charismatic," she writes. "But at my first dinner party with his three oldest friends and their wives, I had to listen to them complain about Clinton. This was before Monica. What was there not to love about Clinton before Monica? Well, I guess if you disagreed with what he stood for, there was a lot not to love. But how could you not agree with what he stood for?"

Of course, as is *pro forma* in such pieces, she pretends to self-knowledge. Marriage to this exotic creature forced her to grow, she says, conceding that maybe she'd been slightly hasty, perhaps even a bit intolerant. She's better now, *wiser*.

But, wait, hold on, don't worry: Everything works out in the end. For she comes home one afternoon to find that her Republican husband has put up a "VOTE OBAMA" sign in their yard.

Yes, *he* is the one who has truly grown, through association with *her*.

Reading it, one only wishes someone had gotten to this miserable patch of doormat that is her husband before it was too late, and forced upon him the advice he so desperately needed to hear: "Listen, we all know it's hard to find the right someone in these harsh environs – but, God, man, for the sake of suffering humanity, don't stop looking!"

We're Here, We're Republican, Get Used To It

REPUBLICANS ARE 45,000 STRONG
IN SAN FRANCISCO, NEARLY
11 PERCENT OF REGISTERED VOTERS!
(ONLY 19 PERCENT BEHIND
"DECLINE TO STATE")

THE DAY I ARRIVE in San Francisco to have dinner with a little cell of local free-thinkers, the lead story on the front page of the town's main paper, the *Chronicle*, is about nearby Berkeley, where city officials, in league with the lunatic anti-war group Code Pink, are trying to shut down the local Marine recruiting center. But for anyone seeking evidence of the true absurdity of life in this lovely corner of the world, the feature story at the bottom of page one will do just as well. It is about the hit movie *Juno*, and a line spoken by its insouciant teenage protagonist to the bourgeois couple hoping to adopt her baby: "You shoulda gone to China. You know, 'cause I hear they give away babies like free iPods."

This amusing bit of dialogue has evidently prompted great anguish in the Bay Area's community of adoptive parents of Chinese babies, who are seizing the moment to join the region's long parade of warmly regarded, self-declared victims. "That's so mean and unfair," as one such is quoted in the story, opining that her children would surely face such unchecked nastiness throughout their lives and she would have to teach them "to be strong."

Welcome to San Francisco, where it's not enough just to be a left-wing maniac – you also have to have no sense of humor.

That's why the get-together with this bunch tonight is so refreshing. Put together by a venture capitalist named David Blumberg and his partner Michel – yes, they're conservative *and* gay – the dinner includes a cross-section of those on the wrong side of the local political divide. Indeed, when I first met David several months back, he told me a story at once remarkably revealing and somehow unsurprising. It was about getting a call back in the fall of 2004 from a *New York Times* reporter seeking an interview. "I'm thinking, 'Great, they want to talk about our firm,'" recalls Blumberg. "But, no, that wasn't it. It seems they'd done a Freedom of Information search on political giving, and found I was the only significant donor to George W. Bush in my entire zip code."

"Welcome to San Francisco," he greets me this evening, "and our own private free speech zone. Everyone here tonight has been through the wars."

They are (with last names omitted, unless otherwise authorized, in the interest of . . . hey, they have to *live* there, we don't):

- Christine Hughes, former Chairman of the San Francisco Republican Party, and her businessman husband Abe.

- Ruvim and Imma, who emigrated to the Bay Area from the former Soviet Union, part of a local Russian-Jewish community of some fifty thousand.

- Alex, a young Internet entrepreneur and his girlfriend Naomi, both fairly recent arrivals from New York.

Literally two minutes after we all gather for cocktails in the living room of David and Michel's townhouse – it's on Haight Street, just a few blocks south of Ashbury – the doorbell rings. A moment later, David ushers a disheveled but very earnest guy of maybe thirty-five into the room.

"We have an unexpected bounty of the neighborhood," he announces. "This gentleman has come to talk to us about – what, exactly?"

"I'm from Environment California," he says, and immediately goes into his spiel about the multiple threats at hand and the "huge wake-up call" and "proactive measures" so desperately needed. "We're doing a lot of lobbying of Congress," he intones, concluding that he is "looking for public comment," and, by the way, "donations."

"So," inquires David politely, "what's the main environmental threat locally we should be concentrating on?"

"Oh, well, there are so many. And every issue contains many sub-issues. Global warming, of course, but that's really more of a symptom. We've got to clamp down on all the industries that are doing damage."

"Have you done any cost-benefit analysis on these 'solutions' to see how they might impact the economy and affect peoples' lives?"

This momentarily stops him. "Well," he offers, "I'm not really trained to talk about that. But we do have a website you can look at."

When the guy's left and we're heading for the dining room, I remark to David that this must have been a plant.

"Actually," he says, laughing, "you never know what's going to show up at the door – you just know it probably won't be respectable. Last Halloween, being extremely conscious of the local sensibilities, we put out our pumpkins, and made sure that the children had healthful treats – peanuts, and raisins, and cashews, all in tamper-proof containers. The whole night we only had three groups. One was one little kid, with five adults – we didn't know if it was 'it takes a village,' or divorces and remarriages, or what. Next, we had two black kids dressed in ski parkas and jeans. I said, 'Where's your costumes?' They said, 'We're skiers.' The last two that came by were these twentysomething, vaguely hippieish types with funky hats and glazed eyes, holding huge garbage bags. I said,

'Aren't you guys kind've old to be trick or treating?' One of them opened his bag and said, 'Actually, we've got something for *you*. Take one, man.' It was full of hash brownies. It was a loss leader marketing campaign – the guys were dealers, using the occasion to drum up future customers." He laughs. "At least they had a little capitalist enterprise. But that's what it's like living around here."

Over dinner, the conversation, on the general subject of being conservative in this most impregnable bastion of left-liberalism, flows freely. What follows, edited for space, are some of the highlights:

> CHRISTINE: I'm a fourth-generation native San Franciscan, but hadn't lived here since shortly after college. So I was surprised, when we came back in 2004, and friends said you can't be vocal about being a Republican in San Francisco; people will spit at you; they'll throw things at you; they'll key your car. I was horrified, because that isn't the city I grew up in.

> MICHEL: In San Francisco, it's actually much easier to be gay than Republican.

> ALEX: I go to tech conferences, and when I describe myself as an "out Republican," certain people are almost envious. They agree with me, but they feel they have to stay closeted.

> CHRISTINE: There are about 45,000 Republicans in the city – we're now less than 11 percent. "Decline to state" is now 30 percent. And that's the reason, the stigma attached to saying you're a Republican.

> DAVID: When I came out as a Republican, friends abandoned me. I got called a fascist, traitor, crazy, insane, a racist. They're totally uninterested in anything that runs counter to their narrative of the way the world works.

The possibility that someone might move to the right because Republicans help the economy grow and they're the ones who *really* help poor people is beyond them.

MICHEL: They'd say it to me: How could David, who's so smart, be a Republican?

DAVID: But, of course, you meet all these new people, who are so much – I was going to say smarter, but it's not exactly that. They're better informed. They look at evidence. People on the left around here don't read the data, and they really don't have any curiosity.

ALEX: The standard view is that the Christian Right sets the entire domestic agenda. But if you ask exactly how the Christian Right is doing this, and what policies they're talking about, they won't go there.

DAVID: The Christian Right, the great bogeyman! Especially here! But that wasn't my experience at all. When I came out as a gay man to my Christian friends, I was sometimes greeted with incomprehension, but always with love and respect – the attitude was: "You're our friend, and that's not going to change." This from the supposed "haters." It was the same with Orthodox Jews. I remember a conversation I had with an Orthodox rabbi where he said, "Tell me you're dating a nice Jewish girl." I said, "Well, I'm dating, but it's not a girl." The rabbi said, "My son, may you be blessed, and may you continue to increase your Jewish practice." He was warm, and kind, and accepting. Would he have preferred that I was straight? Absolutely. But he made sure that the comment he was able to comfortably make was positive. I had only one friend on the right who had any kind of problem. He said, "You shouldn't have children, it's not fair to the kids," and even that was a pragmatic argument that I could respect. In fact, I totally agree it's better for children to have a father and a mother, because there's a natural balance there.

MICHEL: You can't replace the mother, the love of a mother.

DAVID: The point is, there's just this amazing lockstep mentality in this city. And if you live here, you'd better have a sense of humor about it. I mean, it's one thing to see someone with a hand-lettered sign that says, "There are no terrorists, we're all being manipulated." Fine, we all know there are maniacs out there who believe that. But around here there are actual billboards, put up by major companies, saying things like, "Don't Make War, Drink Our Vodka Instead." They know their audience. Sometimes, for the hell of it, I'll go to the farmer's market in the Ferry Building on Sunday morning wearing my t-shirt that says, "Except For Ending Slavery, Fascism, Communism, and Nazism, War Has Never Solved Anything." And people will glance at it, and, thinking it's anti-war, give a clenched fist or say, "Right on!" "Hold on," I'll say, "Take your time. Read it again."

ALEX: They literally can't process it!

RUVIM (*laughs*): "How can this be? Is he saying war can be good?

ALEX: I used to wear one in high school that said, "Gun Control Is Being Able to Hit Your Target." One girl couldn't take it anymore, she finally erupted, "You're so conservative, I want to hit you!"

RUVIM: Imma and I both grew up in the Soviet Union – I emigrated as a political refugee in '79. When our son comes home from school, he will often start repeating the latest piece of political correctness. When we tell him we don't necessarily think this way, he's amazed, because no one else he meets ever questions it.

IMMA: Of course, it's quite familiar to us, this kind of thing.

RUVIM: Because this is how we grew up in the Soviet Union. There are things you hear at home, but know you are never supposed to repeat at school. I never thought we would have to do this with our kid in the United States.

DAVID: You definitely have to self-censor. I had friends with whom I once felt I could discuss anything, and now there are whole vast subject areas where I know I just can't go there. Aside from basic political differences, this place is the land of the "chronically offended." Everyone wants to lay claim to some kind of victimhood. Even non-humans. There was a resolution before the Board of Supervisors, offered by Chris Daley, the most left-wing member, declaring that if you live in San Francisco, you're merely your pet's guardian, no longer its owner. Pets have independent spirits, they should be free, not slaves!

RUVIM: The next step will be that my dog sues me!

CHRISTINE: I'm not sure that one went anywhere. But that's what the Board of Supervisors does, it makes these grand proclamations, basically declaring something is so. Actually, it's the kind of thing that emboldened me to become a Republican activist in this city. I said, "This is where I was born and raised. This is a democracy. I'm not going to let anyone tell me what I can and cannot believe in." The Board of Supervisors in place now are all "progressives" – that's the word they use, because they don't want to be called liberals. Well, they've steadily progressed this city backward.

ABE: One of the supervisors wanted to permanently ban the Blue Angels from flying over the city, which had been a yearly event.

CHRISTINE: That was one of the things that we, as Republicans, organized around. Another was a move by a couple of members of the School Board to eliminate the JROTC from the public schools. One of these guys had been elected to the board after being in Canada as a draft dodger, then coming back and going to federal prison. Well, I personally got all over this one, sending out newsletters, mobilizing media. Then they tried to ban the Marines' Silent Drill Team, which was touring the country, denying them permission to be photographed on the Golden Gate Bridge. Some public affairs woman actually proclaimed: "Not on my bridge will you have that freakin' military with their guns!"

RUVIM: The Russian community went totally nuts over that one. Big time.

CHRISTINE: Well, we took these three incidents, and started getting all this publicity about how San Francisco is anti-military, anti-"our troops." It drove the mayor crazy. He started screaming and yelling. But that's what you've got to do, shine light on these things. The truth is, we've got very serious problems in this city that go far beyond all this nonsense. We have 744,000-plus residents, with the number continually in decline, yet our budget this year is $6.6 billion! Higher than Los Angeles or San Jose. . .

ABE: Which has three million people.

CHRISTINE: You look at how it's spent, and your head starts spinning! All the mayor's programs are directed at the homeless or the impoverished, who represent about 10 percent of the population. It's insane.

ABE: This city spends $130,000 annually per homeless person. That includes the cost of the personnel, the housing, the infrastructure. If they just gave each of those people eighty thousand, they'd save fifty.

DAVID: When [Mayor] Gavin Newsom first ran, a lot of us supported him. He was going to represent a new direction for San Francisco. And the guy he was running against, Matt Gonzalez, was one of those Communists to the manner born.

CHRISTINE: He ran on the Green Party.

DAVID: Can you believe it – we actually had a cocktail party in this house to help raise money for Newsom. He gave us each a book, *Twenty-First Century City* by Stephen Goldsmith, the conservative Republican mayor of Indianapolis. He told us he was for competition and privatization. He said the unions are just strangling the government, and we have to start outsourcing government services. What an incredible snow job! As soon as he was elected, he tacked hard left.

CHRISTINE: Twenty-seven thousand people work for the city and county of San Francisco, roughly 6.7 percent of the entire workforce.

RUVIM: I know I keep repeating myself – but it's almost like the Soviet Union.

CHRISTINE: In 2007–2008, we spent more per capita than any other city in the country! We spent more that the entire state budget for twenty-two states. San Francisco spends 52 percent more per capita than San Jose and almost twice as much as Oakland.

DAVID: And if you work for the city for five years, you get to retire with full health benefits. And we haven't even gotten to the crime.

CHRISTINE: We have a major problem in this city with homicide, and it's only getting worse. The homicide rate is escalating even in "good" areas of the city.

NAOMI: I have a friend from Berkeley who was shot and killed here. After living in Manhattan, I'm terrified.

DAVID: Wealthy cities generally don't have this kind of homicide rate. If you adjust for for socioeconomic status, we have the highest homicide rate in the country – higher than cities like Detroit.

CHRISTINE: I don't know what it is about the people who live here. Maybe because it's such a beautiful place – but it's amazing there's not more outrage. Crime is rampant. The public school system is a joke. We have almost no middle class anymore.

DAVID: Of course, part of the crime problem is that there's such incredible antipathy toward the police, so they get almost no cooperation. Since the police are supposedly racist, and all the rest, people don't report things to them. Then there's the attitude toward drugs. They've fought nine years to get the drug dealers off the streets in this neighborhood, and now we've given them storefronts – otherwise known as "medical marijuana dispensaries." There are five within walking distance of here.

CHRISTINE: What an amazing fraud that is. These doctors just hand out prescriptions to anyone.

DAVID: You've never seen so many twenty-two-year-old skateboarders with glaucoma in your life! So they buy their medical marijuana, and resell it on the street. You see all these cars double parked, so I said to a cop, "Listen, I know you can't stop them from selling marijuana, but can you at least stop people from double parking?" I'm thinking, you know, "small victories." He says, "Oh, no, sir, I'm sorry, we can't do anything. Because if we say anything, they'll accuse us of being racist."

ALEX: The black dealers can out-compete the white dealers, because the white dealers have a greater chance of being arrested.

CHRISTINE: I can't stand the governance of this city. It drives me crazy every single day.

What we need in this city is a Giuliani.

DAVID: That's what we were hoping Newsom might be. If not quite a Republican, as close as we were likely to get. Instead, he completely screws up and gets reelected with 70 percent of the vote!

CHRISTINE: Last time the Republicans didn't even field a serious candidate.

RUVIM: As a fellow Russian Jew put it to me, the Messiah will come before we get a Republican elected mayor of San Francisco!

CHRISTINE: We only have one elected Republican in the entire city and county, and that's on the BART board – the Bay Area Rapid Transit.

ALEX: There's a certain logic there: A city that believes Republicans are fascists lets a Republican on the agency responsible for making the trains run on time. Sorry, a bit of gallows humor.

DAVID: It's almost impossible to believe now, but for generations San Francisco was a Republican city. It was clean, had the best schools in the state, a very low crime rate, and in general was a very civil place. I can remember even when I was a kid, women wore gloves and hats.

CHRISTINE: The last Republican mayor was George Christopher, in the early Sixties.

DAVID: Of course, that's when everything changed, in the Sixties and Seventies, and San Francisco became the world capital of narcissism and self-indulgence. It's still a lovely city in many respects – but, really, it's lovely because of capitalism, and the Republicans who built it. They were people who believed in free markets and rights and responsibilities. Since Dianne Feinstein was mayor and put in rent control, we've been in steady decline. This whole neighborhood used to be single-family homes – one family built this home in 1884, and they lived here for a hundred years, staying even when Haight-Ashbury was in its heyday. But most of the lovely old family homes around here were split up into apartments, and there are very few families left. Now this is one of the least family-friendly cities in the country.

CHRISTINE: When tourists come into this city, they see a different place than we do, because it's still one of the most beautiful cities in the world. But even they are having a harder and harder time ignoring how much it's deteriorated – all the graffiti, and the homeless everywhere, and the filth. If you're in high heels, you take your life in your hands because of the potholes. And I predict it'll have to get worse before it gets better.

* * *

Later, I stand with my hosts at the door as the guests are leaving, thanking them for their participation. The Russians, Ruvim and Imma, are the last to go, lingering a few minutes after the rest. I ask Ruvim about his references to the Soviet Union, and whether, in fact, he might have been somewhat overstating things.

He thinks about it a moment, and then, unexpectedly, he laughs. "Let me tell you a little story," he says. "When I was young, my grandfather lived in our home. He was the chief rabbi of Leningrad for thirty-three years, not counting time in prison camps, and he had a much younger cousin, a decorated war hero and a devoted Communist, who would sometimes visit us. My grandmother was an ardent Zionist, and had a very low threshold of patience for this guy. But my grandfather – I'll never forget it – he would sit and listen and smile, never argue with him. It was almost as if he pitied him. Having seen it all, he had the wisdom to know you can't win arguing with a maniac. That was his wisdom." He laughs again. "It was good preparation for living in San Francisco."

My Wife Tries Again – *and Fails* – to Bridge the Gap

REACHING OUT TO A BELOVED
LIBERAL SPIRITUAL HEALER

I KEEP TELLING HER: They won't listen! They're impervious to reason! They don't care! Forget it – spare yourself the grief! And she of course knows this is true. But then she gets in these moods and starts thinking, "It's not possible, they can't really be as narrow and utterly closed-minded as they seem!"

I'd been aware that she'd come across a book at some sale by a New Age type named Marianne Williamson, and was even aware that, surprisingly enough, she thought it had some interesting things to say.

But I had no idea that when she finished it she was in one of those moods, and would actually reach out to the woman.

Believe me, I'd have tried to stop her.

Dear Marianne,

I picked up your book *Everyday Grace* at a library sale and found much of it truly wonderful, wise, and thoughtful. However, what I did not find wonderful (and certainly neither wise nor thoughtful) was its politics. Your books would have a good deal more spiritual resonance if they didn't at every turn reflect the parochial LA–Hollywood left-liberal agenda. But my guess is that you're not even aware of your biases and prejudices; that's just the water you swim in, the air you breathe, the way it is.

We're roughly the same age, and I, too, have been a spiritual seeker for much of my adult life, particularly in the last decade or so. I, too, started out on the left – I was a philosophy major at Berkeley. But along the way I had to abandon many of my prejudices because my comfortable Sixties assumptions just didn't work in the real world. This is probably why I find your instinct for government solutions so distressing. I remember my father, a Southern Democrat who would have cut off his arm before pulling the lever for a Republican, saying in disbelief of his close friend Arley Tripp "he's the most decent person in the world – will do anything for anyone – and he's a Republican!" He just could not reconcile that decency with his friend's politics. He never realized that Arley's decency and his politics were of a piece; his friend simply believed that people – neighbors, friends, family, not the state – were what you turned to when you needed help. In Arley's world, you certainly didn't turn to government first.

Both Arley and my father are dead now, but I think Arley is particularly vindicated. No matter how well intended (and they always are!), government solutions to so many problems metastasize into stagnant bureaucracies that end up serving no one well – and allow people to think whatever the problem is, it's up to government to deal with it. It breeds moral complacency and a hand-washing indifference. Do you know that the level of charitable giving in European countries is far, far, far below that of the United States? Few give personally in Europe because they've been conditioned to believe that charity is a government, not personal, responsibility.

And the levels of European-government giving are lower than individual giving in the United States. When you combine what our government gives with what individuals give, the United States is the most generous country on earth by far! The tsunami disaster in Indonesia a few years ago is a casebook study, and I recommend you look at the numbers, because it's incredibly illuminating. And, if I may say so, totally at odds with what you seem to be agitating for throughout the book.

I hope this isn't out of line, but perhaps you might consider moving (for a while, anyway) to another part of the country and surrounding yourself with different sorts of people. I think a broadened perspective would enrich your books.

Anyway, believe it or not, this is a fan letter – your book hit so many inspiring notes for me that the political assumptions that crept in were especially discordant and too often kept it predictable and earthbound.

Sincerely,
Priscilla Turner

When I googled Marianne Williamson, I learned, among other things, that she is "a spiritual activist" and "founder of The Peace Alliance, a grassroots campaign supporting legislation currently before Congress to establish a United States Department of Peace." Maybe that's why she couldn't find the time to make even a perfunctory reply to my wife's letter.

Broadcasting from the Occupied Territory

LEFT-OF-CENTER VIEWERS in Madison, Wisconsin – which is to say, just about *everyone* in Madison, Wisconsin – are regularly subjected to their own mini-version of Abu Ghraib, in the form of commercials featuring local conservative talk radio star Vicki McKenna. One of the spots casts the sassy McKenna as Madison's mayor, giddily vetoing one dumb, free-enterprise-suffocating piece of legislation after another, before waking from her dream in bed in her Reagan t-shirt. Another has her demolishing a liberal caller, then breezily remarking that "every now and then you just have to shake your head at the idiots." In a third, her target is that evergreen liberal cure-all for social chaos, midnight basketball, as the announcer intones, "She's the voice of reason in a city of chaos."

Then there's her personal favorite. It opens with the printed words "Vicki McKenna relaxing after a long day dealing with Madison liberals," then cuts to McKenna on her living room couch watching a video of Saddam Hussein's execution. "Oh," she concludes dreamily, "I wish I could've been there."

"That one didn't go over well," she says, laughing, in her cramped office at her WIBA studio. "No one would even take the spot. It's too *controversial*. I mean, here I am, cheering on the death of one of the most tyrannical, homicidal monsters in the history of the world, and in Madison, the *appropriate* reaction is to feel bad he's dead."

If Madison's not the hardest left college town in America, it's in an ongoing fight with Berkeley for the title – with Ann Arbor nipping at their heels – and a day spent with McKenna is an in-depth tutorial on the lunacies of daily life in Wisconsin's capital city. As whip-smart as she is outspoken (not to mention pretty damn good looking), wired on adrenaline and an endless stream of diet Cokes and hand-rolled cigarettes ("What, I'm going to pay a dollar extra in tax, so they can fund an ever-expanding Wisconsin government, when we've got a structural deficit of over two billion dollars?"), McKenna, at thirty-nine, has a take on the town that is two parts bemused incredulity and one part affectionate contempt.

"I can't count how many times my car's been keyed around here – the wrong bumper sticker is an open invitation for that, if not worse. In 2004, a couple of folks had Bush–Cheney signs in their yard and someone took weed killer and made giant swastikas on their lawns." She offers a what-can-you-expect smile. "It's always the Nazis, and the police are always using 'Gestapo tactics.' Only in Madison could a former mayor, a radical who once ran for office virtually as a communist, be regarded as the conservative candidate – because he was getting LARD [Landlord Real Estate Development] money. Because, obviously, profit is *evil*."

This leads McKenna to the matter of Madison's municipal government, a bottomless treasure trove of unintentional comedy. "We don't have money to mow the parks or fill the potholes, and we certainly don't have money for the cops we need. So what does our city council spend its time on? We vote to pull out of Iraq, and to impeach the president and the vice president. We debate the Tibetan flag, and the Palestinian right of return, and whether to embrace Rafa in Gaza as our sister city, and whether it's right to give hungry people a turkey on Thanksgiving, because it's violence against the bird. Speaking of which, right now we're debating urban chickens.

"If it has nothing to do with city governance, we've tackled it. We fund a hooker rehabilitation program here in Madison. No hookers have *been* rehabilitated, mind you, because they don't *want* to be rehabilitated, but so what? We've got empowerment programs for girls – they're probably giving 'em contraceptive advice at age six. We've got a Mung bingo program – because, don't you know, it's important for the Mung community to have bingo options, like I'm sure they had back in Laos. But try getting a business going here and all you run into is obstacles. This is the nanny state on steroids, the total micromanagement of people's lives."

This off-the-cuff rant will begin to convey a sense of McKenna's show – or two shows, actually, since she broadcasts two hours in the morning to Milwaukee in addition to her three-hour home-town Madison show in the afternoon. She speaks without notes for five, six, seven minutes at a stretch, at once enormously good-humored and incredibly passionate.

"Maybe my favorite government expenditure of all," she adds now, "is for Madison's community television station. They have a show called 'Cooking With Bob.' You never actually see Bob. What you do see, for three hours, is various objects cooking and melting over a rotisserie – a shoe, a plastic bottle, whatever, and periodically words will flash on the screen. Words with deep meaning, like 'blood' or 'war' or 'oil.' People think it's a cool Madison thing. Bob is a local hero, and people treasure this retarded show."

McKenna concedes that occasionally – all right, more than occasionally – she runs into aspects of the Madison mentality that are harder to laugh away. Back in 1970, for instance, in one of the most appalling acts of violence of a misbegotten era, Sterling Hall, site of the University of Wisconsin Physics Department, was bombed by radicals, resulting in the death of thirty-three-year old Robert Fassnact, a post-doctoral student and father of three young children. The chief bomber was one Karleton Armstrong, who was arrested after a year and a half on the lam and sentenced to twenty-three years, of which he served only seven.

"When he got out," says McKenna, "he opened up a sandwich shop called The Radical Rye, and the upper part of the place was called The Che's Lounge. Cute, huh? This guy did very well embracing corporate greed. But what's truly stomach-turning is that, though he's never expressed remorse for what he did, in Madison he was never ostracized in any way – he was embraced. And every year on the anniversary of the bombing, old Madisonians come out to remember that day, and talk about the good times protesting the war, and no one even remembers the name of the victim."

Still, both on the air and off, McKenna is the polar opposite of downbeat. As she says, "The healthiest way to look at this town – I'm talking mental health – is as comedy. These people are *craaazy*. My basic approach is to mock them, and otherwise assert intellectual superiority. Because frankly, when you come down to it, they have no arguments beyond name-calling. It's just that they live in a universe where they're never challenged – ever. So when they are, they're kind of helpless."

She pauses, smiling, beneath a large golden bust of Ronald Reagan on the shelf above her desk, an award from Americans for Prosperity. "I've actually proposed a 'Slap-the-Crap-Out-of-'Em' ordinance, mandating that whenever anyone says something especially dumb, they get a big fat whap against the head. I tell you, it's like the show writes itself."

Born into a conservative Catholic family – "My father used to describe Rush as too liberal" – by high school McKenna thought of herself as a leftist. "I had a teacher who said it was anti-intellectual to be patriotic. We loved her – she was very cool, watched R-rated anti-war movies with us. In college, I declared sociology as a major, and it was all downhill from there. I remember this kid came up to me, an econ major, and he says, 'How can you defend Communism? How can you defend Che Guevara murdering thousands of people?' It threw me for a loop for about five seconds – then I actually heard myself say, 'Well, sometimes you gotta die for the truth.' Years later, I still go red when I think about saying that – especially having talked to Cuban Americans who battled sharks to escape that regime."

She began to figure things out "when I began paying taxes," and over the next several years found herself transformed from "a ridiculous, ignorant Marxist, to a standard liberal Democrat, to, around the time of the Contract with America" – a short, self-mocking laugh – "the pistol-packing free-thinker I am today."

After getting into radio, she arrived at Madison's news-talk station as assistant news director in 1994. But landing a job as a daily talker took some doing. "My general manager said: 'You want to do political talk? But you're a Republican, right?'" "Exactly," she countered, "it's an underserved market – and it's sure not gonna be hard to get someone to pay attention." Still, playing it safe, they initially paired her with a liberal co-host. "I shouldn't speak ill, but it was torture. This fellow would actually quote Maureen Dowd's opinion pieces as fact. You just wanted to take a baseball bat and go *whap*. I finally threatened to quit and sell cars."

When she got the solo show, it took off quickly. "Sure enough, there was an underserved market, filled with people who had under-expressed frustration. Actually, we all know each other – we have secret knocks and secret handshakes."

Indeed, McKenna's three hours of daily airtime are a port in the storm for Madison's beleaguered community of conservatives. "Broadcasting from the Occupied Territory," as her announcer intones when the show returns from a break, or, "From the Belly of the Beast," or simply, "Planet Madison, on the Dark Side of the Moon." The message is always the same: Here, at long last, is a voice of sanity in a city that has lost its collective mind. Her show leads the ratings in her time slot, doing especially well with older people and the key demographic of young men. During some broadcasts, in addition to calls, she receives as many as two hundred emails.

This afternoon, for my benefit, she asks listeners to come up with a single word that sums up Madison. Almost instantly, the message board lights up and the emails start coming. Among the suggestions: "Bizarroland," "unhinged," "Orwellian," "wacked," "surreal," "liberalicious," "draconian," "fubar." One caller suggests "Kafkaesque," adding, "I tell you, Vicki, I listen to some of the stuff that comes out of Madison, and it's no more surprising than going to bed a man and waking up a cockroach."

"I love that," she replies, laughing. "Sometimes I've just gotta lick my chops at the low-hanging fruit available to me here."

But today, as every day, her impromptu monologues and rants are the heart of the program. On the agenda this afternoon:

· *Liberty v. the religion of environmentalism:* "Green, green, green. Green make-up. Green cars. Green cleaning products. The latest in green is eating bugs. . . . What happened to individual liberty? Choice doesn't matter when it comes to what kind of freakin' light bulb I want to buy or whether I throw my pop can in a garbage can versus a recycling bin. Does choice only matter when it comes to killing a baby? . . . Look, I don't want to pave the forests. I like the deer and the bears and the plants. I like the bugs and snakes and all the critters. But I am not sacrificing my life and livelihood to make sure that we might some day be able to prevent a miniscule increase in the global mean temperature that may or may not have an adverse effect on the bugs and the bears and the trees. . ."

· *On fighting back:* "It's fine to sign a petition, but it's not enough. You need to *blanket* the fax machines. You need to *make* [elected representatives] pay attention. You need to obnoxiously *annoy* them. Wake up every day and think like a leftist. When the average person wakes up in the morning, it's, 'I wonder if I can get five extra minutes.

I gotta get the kids to school. I wonder if I'll get to work on time.' When leftists wake up, before they hit that snooze alarm, they're thinking of how they can move their agenda forward."

· *On social dysfunction in the inner cities:* "I stopped being a liberal when I stopped making excuses for people. . . . Does it help a woman to make excuses for why she decided to hook up with four guys and have five kids and not marry a single one of them? Somewhere along the line we stopped being allowed to criticize that person for her bad decisions – decisions that are almost sure to have disastrous consequences for her children. We're always being lectured by the liberals about how we need to do the right thing by kids. . . . Well, you can't have an economy with just people who breathe through their mouth and have a pulse. . . . I have boundless sympathy for these kids. I have no sympathy for their mothers – none! I've got a proposal. We start a brand new class in the public schools, running from kindergarten all the way through high school. It's called 'Middle-Class Values.' And Mom's got to take the class, too – because she fails to understand what deferred gratification is. She's living her life miserable bastard to miserable bastard, and she's training her kids to do the exact same thing. And if you don't understand deferred gratification, you will never be able to participate in America – you just won't."

But the issue dominating the show today is the just-announced closing of a GM plant in Janesville, Wisconsin, which will result in the loss of as many as four thousand jobs. Vicki feels the workers' pain, sort of, but what she mainly feels is disgust at the moral corruption, flat-out incompetence, and by-the-book liberalism that led to this disaster.

"What the state of Wisconsin refuses to accept is that it gets in its own way!" she declares. "It gets in the way of retaining manufacturing, of attracting new manufacturing. . . . Why in the heck does the state of Wisconsin have a state-only global warming task force exploring alternative energy options that hamstring manufacturing? Why are we going out of our way to roll back mercury emissions 90 percent?

"Wind and solar is not going to power a plant! It will not help anyone who does not have a college degree. . . . Texas, Indiana, Tennessee, Alabama – these are destinations for business. Wisconsin used to be on that list! . . . Businesses will always cite the same things: tax climate, regulatory climate, legal climate. It's simple. You don't need Milton Friedman raised from the dead to come here and give us advice! We chased people out, and hung a sign on the door that says, 'Please don't come.'"

Immediately after this, she fields a call from William, an electrical engineer looking to start a business but running into the local legal obstacles and general anti-capitalist crap seemingly designed to kill the entrepreneurial spirit.

"Oh, stop it!" exclaims McKenna, "It's Madison, for heaven's sake! Business? Are you actually trying to create *profit?*"

"I am."

"*Jobs?* Are you trying to diversify the tax base? And you're trying to do this in Madison?"

"I am."

"Wait, let me ask you a question. Are you interested in turning corn into gasoline?"

"No."

"Are you interested in wind power?"

"No."

"Solar power?"

"No."

"Are you interested in creating stem cells?"

"No."

"I'm sorry, you can't play."

McKenna sees her mission – "in addition to the profit motive, let's not forget that" – as helping to give local conservatives some spine. "They're like political battered women around here, a lot of them. They've been beaten back so long, they're afraid to step out of line even a little bit. They won't even admit what they are. Sure, it's true, people may not like you. I've been called 'Attila the Hun,' a Nazi, a Neanderthal, pick your pejorative. But, you know what – the thing to do is embrace it. Because refusing to be defensive and actually fighting back, that's what really drives 'em nuts. They literally don't know what to do. Some of these old hippies call up and they hate my guts so much, you swear they're gonna have a stroke and drop dead on the phone."

She pauses in mid-rant, and smiles. "I'm just not big on backing off. It's not like I seek conflict; I'll usually try to defuse the situation. But if that doesn't work, I can be crazier than they can."

By way of example, she recalls an episode, circa the fall of 2004. "I was pulling my truck into a parking lot for one of those big-box pet stores, and realized too late that I'd accidentally taken this woman's parking spot. So she finds another spot, and I see her marching over. I'm all ready to say, 'Sorry, you're right,' when it turns out that's not it at all. She's seen my Bush sticker, and feels compelled to call me a child-killer. So I pop down the tail of my truck, pat it, and say, 'Have a seat. If we're gonna debate the war, let's do it in a reasonable manner.' But she refuses, just keeps yelling. 'Look,' I say, 'it's a beautiful day, please sit down and debate the war with me.' She keeps yelling. So finally I say, 'Fine, let's go inside the pet store, and you keep yelling – but I guarantee you, when it comes to crazy, I can outlast you.' So we go into the store and the tables turn. Now I won't leave her alone. I start shadowing her through the place, very creepy, really freaking her out – talking at her, whistling, whatever. She'd turn the corner of an aisle and there I'd be, saying in this eerily calm voice, 'Oh, you have a cat – now I know even more about you.' She ends up fleeing from the store, without even buying anything."

She smiles, looking every bit as pleased as she did watching Saddam take the drop. "I tell you, giving it right back to an angry liberal, there's nothing like it."

Safety in Numbers

THERE ARE SAFE HOUSES
TO BE FOUND EVEN
IN MADISON

IN EVEN THE MOST forbiddingly left-leaning of locales, there are places where conservatives can find refuge among their own. Even in Madison. Vicki McKenna, with an assist from her listeners, compiled the following list of safe houses in that inhospitable political clime.

VILLA TAP (2302 Packers Ave): Conservatives welcomed with open arms. Owner Al Tedeschi fears no liberal! When Mayor Dave Cieslewciz ran for reelection in 2006, Al flew the Soviet Flag at his bar in his honor.

LE TIGRE LOUNGE (1328 S Midvale Blvd): Owner and frequent bartender Steve Josheff (who always bartends in a shirt and tie) keeps an 8 × 10″ photo of Rush Limbaugh over the bar. 'Nuff said.

BABE'S BAR AND GRILL (5614 Schroeder Rd): West-siders seeking fellow sufferers with whom to gripe about the Madison insanity can always find them at Babe's. Owner Lynn Hacker helped lead the valiant (but, of course, losing) fight against Madison's smoking ban.

BENNETT'S MEADOWOOD COUNTRY CLUB (2009 Freeport Rd): When the smoking ban was enacted, owner Gene Bennett rolled a trailer over to the bar, installed a giant cigarette on top of it, and labeled it the "smoking lounge," complete with heat and ashtrays.

ESQUIRE CLUB (1025 N Sherman Ave): Old-time supper club. The banquet hall is big enough to host a good-sized meeting, and is frequently the location of the conservatives' post-election parties. Owner John Cavanaugh is a great friend of business in Madison (and there aren't many!).

WIGGIE'S BAR (1901 Aberg Ave): Great, working-class bar owned by old-school union guy Dave Wiganowsky, one of the few conservatives on the Dane County board, and a great supporter of common-sense conservatism and veterans.

KENNEDY MANOR (1 Langdon St Dining): Owned by long-time Madison conservative businessman and Ward Connerly pal Fred Mohs. The manager, Mike Thiessen, is a *huge* conservative. The great food is just a bonus.

VFW POST 1318 (133 E Lakeside): Lots of military friendlies, and since it's a private facility, you *can* smoke there! The more patriotic you are, the better they like it!

Ditto VFW 8483 (5737 County Rd Cv).

DELANEY'S STEAKHOUSE (449 Grand Canyon Dr): In the bar area, the conversation routinely veers to the right. And the owner Jim Delaney loves to join in.

KURT'S ON MAIN (1902 Main St, Cross Plains, Wisconsin): Right outside Madison – meaning you can still smoke! Folks from all over the county come to Kurts to gripe openly without fear of liberal retribution.

And a few proudly conservative Madison businesses:

PARK STREET SHOE REPAIR (609 S Park St): Owner George Fabian does good shoes *and* gives great conversation.

Pet World Warehouse Outlet (2148 W Beltline Hwy): They hang a *giant* flag ribbon to show support for the troops.

The Ammo Box (1110 N Bristol Street, in nearby Sun Prairie, Wisconsin): Owner, who goes by "Tryg," eats liberals for breakfast. And he carries a Glock 17 on his hip.

Shoot-Out over the Holiday Table

OR, LEAVE THE GUN, TAKE THE
TURKEY LEG, AND TAKE YOUR
DAMN POLITICS WITH YOU

ONE AFTERNOON in the spring of 2007, my father and step-mother were heading from their Manhattan home to Connecticut when my father started feeling ill. My father is no kid, so my step-mother, who takes splendid care of him, and is a big worrier, anyway, called ahead. By the time they reached their destination, an EMT crew was waiting.

"How do you feel?" asked the head EMT guy.

"I don't feel so good."

"What hurts you?"

"It hurts me that George Bush is president."

My father told me that story himself the next day, describing with relish how the EMT guy hesitated a moment, then cracked up.

My father is one of those rare souls fortunate enough to make his avocation, genius-level kidding around, his profession. He writes not merely well, but funny, and has for many years made a healthy living doing so, starting in radio and early television, later moving on to Broadway and films.

Though he is certainly capable of seriousness (indeed, the meld-ing of comedy and drama is largely what makes his best work emotionally effective), it is not his natural state, and even on those occasions that call for it, he will often puncture the mood with a spontaneous quip.

There are times, as we have seen, when my father will joke about politics, as he does about everything else. Only, in this case, not really – not, that is, when it comes to matters of substantive policy or controversial figures on the national scene.

He is, as he will proudly declare to almost anyone, strangers included, a man of the left. As for so many of his background – first-generation New York Jewish – this is a set of doctrinal beliefs so deeply held they add up to a secular religion. Principal among these beliefs is that while the liberal stance is not always right – often it is insufficiently to the left – the conservative position is, by definition, on every issue, a moral abomination.

As one might imagine, this is a source of some friction between us.

Plenty of others are in this same situation, of course. The Thanksgiving Day Problem, it might be called, though that glib shorthand trivializes what for some can be a source of real and lasting pain.

After all, most of us are born into our politics, and breaking with them is breaking with intellectual and moral tradition. Even as a little kid in the Fifties, I knew that Adlai Stevenson was a man of brilliance and insurmountable integrity, someone whose name was spoken with reverence in our home; Ike was, at best, a bumbling dummy. But it was only when I hit sixth grade that I began to grasp that my parents were a lot more fervent in their commitment to "progressive" ideas, as even then they were known, than the usual run of suburban liberals. That was the year I had as my teacher Mr. Hubley, and if it was strange and curious enough to have a male teacher, what was even stranger, as well as pretty exciting, was Mr. Hubley's determination to set us moving along life's proper path. This was a guy who had strong views about just about everything, and he saw it as his role to spread them. By the end of the second week, we'd heard all about the evils of Communism. He not only gave us the key to the proper spelling of Khrushchev – "when in doubt, always put in an 'h'" – but clued us in to the fact that he was "a cold-blooded murderer." Even worse, at least to those of us who hoped for nothing more in our lives than to one day possess a Corvette, "in Russia, you can go for your car in the morning and find it gone – because you don't own it, the State does."

Never before had I been so jazzed by school. But it was hard not to sense that when I shared Mr. Hubley's insights with my parents, they didn't exactly rush to endorse them. I distinctly remember one evening at dinner when I was quoting Mr. Hubley – this time on the Chinese Communist leadership – when, looking especially pained, they explained that you also had to consider that before Mao and his sidekick Chou en-Lai came on the scene, Chinese children were starving by the *millions*.

Thus began my home schooling phase in geopolitics, with my father cast as master teacher. When, just a year later, I got the plum assignment in seventh-grade history to debate on behalf of John F. Kennedy against Robert Sachs as Nixon's stand-in, my father carefully prepped me the night before. One bit of advice served me especially well: "Remember, if you don't know what to say, just ask: 'What about Alger Hiss?'" It worked beyond my wildest dreams. Though I had only the vaguest notion of who Alger Hiss was – i.e., some totally innocent guy Nixon had sent to prison for doing absolutely nothing – the line sent my teacher's head bobbing and he soon declared me the winner.

There was a lesson there, and I quickly learned it: to be left-of-center was not merely to regard oneself as good and moral and on the right side of history; it was usually to be rewarded by whatever Powers That Were, starting, in this case, with my father.

Sure, I could give him hefty doses of teenage grief. I'll never forget the evening I discovered in the bottom of a filing cabinet the diary he'd written as a fifteen-year-old. It was amazingly erudite, full of references to Shakespeare and Twain, but what grabbed me were his comments about Sacco and Vanzetti, those iconic heroes of the left, who at the time were awaiting execution for a murder that protesters worldwide insisted was a frame-up. Wonder of wonders, in the pages of the diary, my adolescent father revealed himself, at least in this regard, as a full-fledged reactionary. He kept complaining about the damage to property and life and limb the protests were causing, insisting the whole brouhaha would be forgotten after the troublemakers were executed; once they were, and there were a few weeks of relative calm, he crowed about how right he had been.

After reading these passages, I proceeded directly to my parents' bedroom, where my father was watching TV.

"Dad," I asked, "do you remember the Sacco and Vanzetti case?"

"Of course I do," he said.

"What did you think about it at the time?"

"I was all for them, of course. I was a good, left-wing kid."

When I read him a few key passages, he reacted, most uncharacteristically, with something very much like rage.

But that was anomalous. Usually we were on exactly the same page, and ever more so as the civil rights and then anti-Vietnam movements picked up steam. When I went off to college, I started out miles ahead of most of my peers in leftist political sophistication; I could quote verbatim from anti-war journalists like Bernard Fall, not to mention Joseph Welch's "Have you no sense of decency?" spiel that helped take down Joe McCarthy.

And so it went through my early adulthood, as I started in on a career where I was writing, often about politics, for the sorts of mainstream liberal publications my father even now reads religiously, and making him proud.

Then I started to move to the right and, I'm afraid to say, nothing has been quite the same between us since.

* * *

Perspective is always useful, and never more so than when it comes to family feuds over politics and ideology. These are matters that go to our definitions of right and wrong, justice, human progress – which is to say, to our very identities as moral beings – and it is altogether reasonable that the passions they inspire would be all the fiercer when it is our own flesh and blood who embrace a worldview diametrically opposed to our own. It's a good bet that at the very first Thanksgiving, in the midst of all that forced bon-homie, some Pilgrim father and son were casting one another dirty looks over someone's alleged insensitivity to the Native American guests; one can imagine caveman families grunting furiously over the Neanderthal version of the nanny state, i.e., whether to share the day's kill with the lazy s.o.b. in the next cave.

You think intra-family fights were bad during Vietnam, or the Clinton impeachment saga, or the Florida recount, or the appearance of Sarah Palin on the scene? Hell, the nation's early history is a near-continuous record of families sundered beyond repair. The Franklins – that would be father Ben and bastard son William – were merely the celebrity version of what during the Revolution was a painful, universal commonplace. Long after the war, the famously good-humored Ben could still talk only with deep bitterness of the kid who'd held the kite and grown up to be one of the colonies' most prominent loyalists, noting "nothing has ever hurt me with such keen sensations, as to find myself deserted in my old age by my only son."

It hardly needs stating that just a few generations later there were innumerable family members with different perspectives prepared, if it came to it, to kill one another. I have before me an exchange of letters from the opening months of the Civil War, between John and Jabez Pratt, a pair of middle-aged businessman brothers, one a Boston abolitionist, the other a Confederate sympathizer in Baltimore. "Dear Brother," writes John, "You are fast

137

driving me to consider that term inappropriate. . . . If you consider me a 'fool and a boor' why so be it. The only answer I have to make is that you are crazy."

"I am advised this morning that you have so far forgotten yourself [and] personal honor," responds Jabez by return post. ". . . May God forgive you for this act of dishonor and personal treason."

It is a slow motion – and, reflecting the civility of the age, restrained – meltdown of what had always been a loving relationship; had they been in the same room, or lived in today's age of instant electronic insult, one or the other might well have ended up in cuffs on the front page of *The New York Post* under the headline "Honor Killing."

Needless to say, these days, too, there are quite a number of families whose members are at odds with one another over politics and culture; occasionally, the differences are so violent that relationships are indeed sundered. On the less-than-tragic end of the spectrum, one friend tells me that he and his wife have had to permanently ban from various holiday tables a cousin with whom he was once close because, as he puts it, "she's now a MoveOn.org and PETA zealot who won't shut up either about Israel's 'crimes' or the suffering of the damned turkey."

But on the other end of the spectrum, a woman whom I know well describes, with considerable feeling, what now seems to be permanent estrangement from her sister. "Obviously, there were other issues," she says, "a lot of it going all the way back to childhood. Who was our parents' favorite, who got away with stuff, all kinds of trivial episodes that still loom large in our joint history. But it was my politics that gave her her most potent ammunition, and, I think, for her, justifies the break. The fact that I'm a Republican – could actually defend Bush and the war, and vote against Obama – was final proof that I am an absolute nightmare of a person. And she's gotten a lot of support for that from others in her circle."

Still, it rarely gets that bad. Even those most firmly in liberalism's sweaty grip realize, on some level, that these are not quite the times that try men's souls, and that the grimmest brother-against-brother stuff is best left to history. While the exchanges may be frequent and sharp, the permanent damage is contained. "We have violent arguments, say just unbelievably horrible things to each other," reports Amy Anderson, of her down-the-line liberal father. "I've told him that he's a flipping dinosaur moron, and it's beyond me how I came from his spawn and can still manage to walk and talk, and slam down the phone. Five minutes later he'll call back with: 'How does the remote work again?'"

My friend Allen told me just the other day that his favorite aunt had lately called him a Nazi for asserting the superiority of American culture – and "then we sat down with the rest of the family and had a terrific time."

Long before "All in the Family" made it explicitly ideological, millions of us instinctively took that hoariest of sitcom clichés to heart: *After all, in the end, we're still family.*

But let's also face the truth that it often takes a real toll. There are many, many cases in which, in spite of everyone's presumed best efforts, the poison continues to linger, as in those eerie World War I battlefield photos after a mustard gas attack. The feelings on both sides are just too intense, or something's been said that simply cuts too close to the bone.

One woman I know, someone with a hard-edged and un-flinching sense of reality reminiscent of Newt Gingrich's, tells of how nearly impossible it's become to maintain communication with her sister, a liberal, Bank Street-trained schoolteacher. "We can hardly talk about *anything* anymore without arguing. Forget politics. She believes in 'creative math' where kids are supposed to figure out the answers on their own. I believe in teaching the basics; I like football and she thinks it's brutal and glorifies competition. These days we can't even talk about the weather, because of global warming."

This is not one of those things that come between my father

and me. A product of the Depression, he's always been an independent, can-do kind of guy, and, to the extent that he's aware of it, he has little use for the touchy-feely-crunchy-wah-wah aspect of the today's leftist worldview. If not for politics and ideology – and yes, I realize that's a fairly broad exception – we'd be on the same page about nearly everything.

As it is – let's put it this way – my father has no idea what I do for a living. Well, no, that's an exaggeration. He knows that I write books and articles, and that I must be making some money at it, because my family doesn't appear to be starving. But he doesn't know what I write, or where, and he doesn't want to.

It's been this way since the publication of my book *How I Accidentally Joined the Vast Right-Wing Conspiracy (and Found Inner Peace)* at the dawn of this century. I didn't tell him that one was coming, either, but since I was slated to do a lot of publicity and it would probably come to his attention either that way or via some other leftist with a big mouth, I decided it was best to let him know. Several days before the official publication date, I handed him a copy of the book. "What's this?" he asked, and, reading the title, seemed physically to recoil.

"Actually, that's not meant to be taken literally," I said, with a forced smile. (No use explaining there *was* no "vast right-wing conspiracy," that it was a Hillary Clinton creation for purposes of Monica-diversion.) "Look," I added, dropping the magic word for added reassurance, "you won't agree with a lot of it, but at least it's *funny*."

This all occurred at around 2:00 on a Saturday afternoon. Before 4:00, he reappeared, book in hand, barely able to contain himself. "You have a lie in here about a friend of mine!"

The reference was to Zero Mostel and a story I told about how Mostel, having been blacklisted, for a while adamantly resisted collaborating with the brilliant director and choreographer Jerome Robbins, who'd "named names." That is, until one day, Mostel needed Robbins to save a show of his, at which point he grandly announced, "We of the left do not blacklist!"

"That's a lie!" my father repeated.

"But, Dad, you told me that story."

"I did not! This book is full of lies."

After that, we scarcely exchanged a word for a year and a half.

Since then it's slowly gotten better, by fits and starts. Given all we do have in common – the Mets, taste in movies, his grandkids – as long as we steer clear of politics, it's generally okay.

Of course, there are still those fits to go with the starts. The worst was the evening a couple of summers ago when I was out to dinner with my father and my stepmother, and the conversation turned to the rape charges against the Duke lacrosse players, which by then had already been discredited everywhere – except in the *Times*.

"What do you think about it?" asked my stepmother, turning my way.

"What do you think he thinks about it?" roared my father. "He's always against black people!"

"Are you accusing me of being a racist?" I demanded.

When he didn't answer, I slid my chair from the table. "Fine," I said, "see you later."

But then an incredible thing happened: My father apologized. He told me that even though I oppose affirmative action and think Al Sharpton and Jesse Jackson are hustlers – well, no, I took that part to be implied – he *knows* I'm not really a racist. And, knowing how hard that was for him, a truly Herculean effort of goodwill, my anger instantly dissipated, replaced by a gush of love.

There have been no explosions of that magnitude in the time since. In fact, there have actually been reports of him making light of his own beliefs. My daughter tells of having dinner with my father and stepmother during the 2008 presidential campaign and listening to him rail once again against the rich and privileged.

"What are you talking about?" asked my eminently common-sensical stepmother. "You're in the top 1 percent of earners in this country."

This stopped my father short, but only momentarily. "Maybe," he allowed, smiling, "but I'm in the *bottom* of the top 1 percent."

Indeed, early on, during the Democratic death match between Obama and Clinton, he and I actually found ourselves on the same side, if for altogether different reasons. He believed Obama was the Messiah. I just wanted to see Hillary destroyed, slowly and painfully. Nonetheless, it reached the point where we were able to exchange views on the race with genuine interest and civility.

Honor thy father, runs the ancient injunction, and I do, enormously, for his wit, and his uncanny optimism, and his overall decency. When he quotes as gospel yet another story he read in *The New York Times*, I also honor him by not mentioning, hard as it is, that we cancelled our subscription to that piece of crap a year ago.

I also bear in mind that, in the end, all this is far tougher for him than it is for me. There is a moment in his best-loved show, *Fiddler on the Roof*, where Tevye confronts the fact that his daughter Chava wants to marry out of the faith. "[C]an I deny my own child?" he agonizes, looking heavenward. "On the other hand, how can I turn my back on my faith, my people? If I try to bend that far, I will break."

I know how deeply my father felt those words, so know how far he has come in finding ways to live with it, if not exactly understand. This is something else I admire, as well as envy – the man's truly uncanny capacity to deal with bad news.

One Sunday morning just a couple of months ago, when my wife and I arrived at his place for brunch, he greeted us with the devastating news that one of his closest friends had just died.

"Oh, Dad, I'm so sorry."

"Yeah, I know," he replied. "They're using it as an excuse not to join us."

Liberalism as a Mental Disorder

A FEW BRILLIANT SOULS
FINALLY MAKE SENSE OF IT ALL!

SOME PEOPLE PICK their health providers by reputation, or on the advice of friends, or out of insurance manuals. Me, I look for congenial politics. My former dentist, dear old Dr. Krachauur, used to dart into a back room while X-rays were being developed to get the latest from Drudge. When I go in once a year for an update on my heart murmur, my heart guy and I almost immediately resume comparing notes on the latest excesses in academia and the wide, warped world of feminism. When my back went out, I found a chiropractor who loathed the oleaginous Robert Byrd almost as much as I did. So you will understand how delighted I was, when I was in the market for a new general practitioner a couple of years back, to come across the following letter to *The New York Sun*, and note that it was signed by a guy with an M.D. after his name, living in a town very near my own.

> On Sunday, I read the lead review in *The New York Times* book section of Philip Roth's latest novel. Nadine Gordimer took the opportunity to engage in some wild, far-left Bush bashing – even though the novel under review had nothing to do with the current political situation.
>
> Thank goodness *The New York Sun* provides real cultural coverage, instead of agenda-driven politically correct cant.

The doc's name was Steven Rittenberg, and it took less than a minute to find him in the local directory and volunteer myself on his answering machine as a patient.

Alas, it was not to be. When he called back and I offered my reason for seeking him out, he laughed, then gave me the bad news: Yes, he was certainly a conservative, but he wasn't that *kind* of doctor. He was a psychiatrist.

What a stunner! Strictly in terms of rarity, this made him infinitely more precious than your average M.D. Mental health professionals are not only overwhelmingly left of center, but tend to come at you with an especially odious brand of arrogant self-certainty. (Remind me to tell you some time about the one sitting next to my wife at a wedding last year.) They, after all, are *mental health professionals*, and who are *you*?

Though many of us can't really see the difference, because so many of them seem to do the same thing, it is important to distinguish between psychiatrists and psychologists. For one thing, there are a great many more psychologists, nearly as many in this country as grains of sand on the beaches of the Hamptons. The membership of the American Psychological Association numbers 148,000, ranging from the competent to outright quacks, these last being in particular demand in the era of the never-ending search for self-esteem and unearned contentment. Psychologists disagree among themselves about many things, but politics is almost never one of them. "When it comes to politics," understates Brooklyn-based clinical psychologist Paul Hymowitz, himself a political moderate, "the American Psychological Association can be counted on to speak with one voice."

Think of that voice as being not unlike that of the men you hear on NPR, self-consciously soft and a tad whiny – the kind of voice, as recent conservative convert David Mamet says, that one day had his "facial muscles tightening, and the words beginning to form in [his] mind: '*Shut the fuck up.*'"

Of course, to their credit, some in the field make it clear that they don't actually despise conservatives. They simply recognize us for what we are: mentally ill.

In fact, in recent years, quite a number of articles and studies by psychologists have lent weight to this. One, appearing in the magazine *Psychology Today*, determined that while liberals, by the tender age of three, "developed close relationships with peers and were rated by their teachers as self-reliant, energetic, impulsive, and resilient," conservatives were already "easily victimized, easily offended, indecisive, fearful, rigid, inhibited, and vulnerable." Thus, concluded the investigating psychologist, conservatives grew up needing "the reassurance of tradition and authority."

Another study established that while conservatives are terrific at the good-German qualities of "neatness, orderliness, duty, and rule-following," they "have less tolerance for ambiguity"; liberals rate high "on openness, intellectual curiosity, excitement-seeking, novelty, creativity for its own sake, and a craving for stimulation like travel, color, art, music, and literature," and are also "more likely to see gray areas and reconcile seemingly conflicting information."

But my personal favorite is the one done by a clutch of Berkeley psych profs. In an article entitled "Political Conservatism as Motivated Social Cognition," they present a startling conclusion, one that bravely confirms what they and everyone they know has been saying for years: Ronald Reagan, Adolf Hitler, Benito Mussolini, and Rush Limbaugh have key psychological traits in common. All are marked by "fear and aggression, dogmatism, and intolerance of ambiguity; uncertainty avoidance; need for cognitive closure; and terror management." Just to be sure no one got the wrong idea, Berkeley also issued a press release, noting that while Joseph Stalin and Fidel Castro are also widely regarded as monsters, and generally seen as left-wing, in fact, in psychological terms, they "might be considered politically conservative in the context of the systems that they defended."

But let's face it: Psychologists, no matter how diligent or gifted, simply don't project the same authority as those lords of the helping professions, psychiatrists. When they speak, especially en masse, all America sits up and takes notice. Indeed, surely the pivotal victory for the gay rights movement was the 1973 decision by the American Psychiatric Association to remove homosexuality from its official list of mental disorders.

However one feels about that decision – and, frankly, it's no skin off my nose – it's a wonder that those who made it were able keep straight faces while saying it had everything to do with medicine and nothing to do with ideology. Right. Same goes for the mass diagnosis performed nine years earlier, as reported on the cover of the then-hip monthly *Fact Magazine* a month before the Johnson–Goldwater election of 1964: "1189 PSYCHIATRISTS SAY GOLDWATER IS PSYCHOLOGICALLY UNFIT TO BE PRESIDENT!"

"The Unconscious of a Conservative: A Special Issue on the Mind of Barry Goldwater," ran the title of the piece within. It declared, in essence, that the GOP candidate had a severely paranoid personality and was psychologically unfit for the high office to which he aspired. The articles in the magazine attempted to support the thesis that Senator Goldwater was mentally ill by citing allegedly factual incidents from his public and private life and by reporting the results of a "poll" of 12,356 psychiatrists, together with a "sampling" of the comments made by the 2,417 psychiatrists.

The reason those words are in quotes is that they are from a brief in the libel suit Goldwater filed against the magazine that went all the way to the Supreme Court. Not that it matters, but Goldwater won his case, with only the Court's two most liberal justices, Douglas and Black, dissenting.

In the universe of elite thought, rarely does a new idea crowd out shopworn and useless but comforting ones, and little has changed over the years since. Get a psychiatrist on the subject of, say, Clarence Thomas, and he's likely to become as emotionally unhinged as his most delusional patient; the guy at the wedding couldn't even say the name, kept referring to him as "Clarence

146

Uncle Thomas." Needless to say, a very high percentage of them suffered also from BDS – Bush Derangement Syndrome.

But here's the encouraging part: That all-too-apt diagnosis was itself coined by a psychiatrist, the estimable Charles Krauthammer, who was an esteemed member of the field before decamping for the even more dubious satisfactions of journalism and commentary.

Indeed, dissenting conservative psychiatrists, though few in number, are a precious resource when their gifts are put to the service of mankind instead of muddle-headed liberalism; founts of uncommon common sense, they do great good in the world.

My friend Sally Satel, a Yale-trained psychiatrist, likewise doubles as a writer, and in that capacity has produced a couple of extremely necessary books, the titles of which say it all: *P.C. M.D.: How Political Correctness is Corrupting Medicine* and, with Christina Hoff Sommers, *One Nation Under Therapy: How the Helping Culture Is Eroding Self-Reliance*.

Yes, she notes good-naturedly, "I'm kind of ostracized in the profession and encounter a fair amount of venom – the attitude is, 'Oh my God, she's a Republican,' and they almost make the sign of the cross. But there's a lot more to life than getting invited to the right parties."

Chicago-based Dr. Lyle Rossiter is even more isolated. But, then, the book he wrote is an even more scathing attack on the ideological foe. It is entitled *The Liberal Mind: The Psychological Causes of Political Madness*. Fittingly, I stumbled upon it by way of an enraged rant by a liberal blogger, essentially saying, "How dare a conservative accuse us of being crazy!" But that's exactly what Dr. Rossiter does, and then some.

A very brief citation should suffice: "Once the liberal neurosis is no longer disguised as a rational political philosophy, it can be analyzed and treated in whatever manner is necessary to overcome symptomatic distress and functional impairment. . . . The condition's major defects in autonomy and mutuality must be addressed. Prominent among them are a basic mistrust of cooperation; false perceptions of victimization; intense envy and underlying shame; a need to vilify and blame others; deficits in self-reliance and self-direction; a marked fear and avoidance of responsibility; infantile demandingness; an intense and often paranoid hostility; a need to manipulate, control, and depend on others; a lack of courage, resilience, and frustration tolerance; and various defects in ego ideals, conscience, and impulse control. Therapy must also address the liberal's self-pathology, especially his immaturity, self-centeredness, and grandiosity; his lack of empathy for and recognition of others; his marked sense of entitlement; and his impaired self-esteem and identity. Educational programs to cure the liberal's ignorance of free-market economics, libertarian political process, constitutional democracy, and the psychology of cooperation rank high among therapeutic priorities."

Yesss! Give it to 'em, Doc, make 'em choke on it!

In fact, in conversation, the University of Chicago-trained Rossiter is surprisingly mild. "Oh, yes," he avers, when I tell him how I found him, "some of my best publicity comes from enraged liberals. But this wasn't written in anger. Basically, I'm a quiet person, I just had to make sense out of something I'd been thinking about for twenty years."

Among the things he'd been thinking about lately, he says, is why there aren't more like him in the field. "Our tradition of psychoanalysis is to increase the capacity for voluntary choice and rational self interest over one's impulses – not to indulge them in self-destructive ways. So you'd think the psychotherapeutic profession would honor the tradition of individualism, which encourages self-responsibility, not whining and blaming and inviting the citizen to become a ward of the state. Instead they embrace this constant victim-villain paradigm, and attack the moral and legal foundations of ordered liberty, and seem ignorant of the documented destructiveness that seem so obvious to some of us – the War on Poverty and other programs that have been so disastrous for individuals and families."

Rossiter adds that while, at times, it can get pretty lonely, he is pleased to hear from people "all over the place, who love what the book says. Finding people on the same wavelength in the midst of all the liberal noise – that makes all the grief worth it."

Among those from whom he's recently heard, he notes in passing, is a fellow psychiatrist, a guy in the New York area named Steve Rittenberg.

Yes, *that* Steve Rittenberg.

We'd only spoken that once, several years before, after I spotted his letter in the paper. When I reach him now we begin to get into the political and biographical particulars. Rittenberg agrees with Rossiter that "given Freud's skeptical view of human nature and utopian thinking," those in their field really ought to know better. "These are people who are supposed to be self-observant and self-aware. But of course their politics is a set of shared religious beliefs, not open to the skeptical scrutiny they profess to believe in. . . . So many colleagues, whom I respect professionally, I just can't talk to anymore. And I guess it's the same with them. They look upon me as if I'm obviously deranged, which" – he pauses, laughs – "in my profession, is not the best reputation to have."

As for his patients, he says, most of them "just assume I share their left-liberal point of view. When I inquire as to why they would make those assumptions, even the question is intolerable for them. How could someone they assume is intelligent even consider alternate explanations for things?"

Then again, Rittenberg makes clear, he has been out of step with his crowd for a long, long time. Starting as a conventional liberal, he began moving rightward during the Vietnam period. "I was in the Navy after my residency, from '67 to '69, and one of my duties as a Navy psychiatrist was to examine kids who were trying to get out of the draft on psychiatric grounds. Often they were Ivy League kids, faking whatever they could, and the contrast between them and some of my other patients – very admirable wounded Marines and Navy guys – was striking. 'Look,' I'd point out to these Ivy League guys, 'if you don't go, some poor kid from West Virginia's going in your place – the very people for whom you claim to have such sympathy.' This didn't bother them at all. I saw those kids for who they really were – what their values were – and my feelings started to change. That kind of selfishness and narcissism posing as principle has been the story of the left ever since."

Trust me, if I'm ever in the market for a psychiatrist in the area, this is *definitely* my man.

I say this even as a serious Mets fan, after reading Rittenberg's blog to discover he loves the Yankees. In fact, even writing on the contrast between Derek Jeter and Alex Rodriguez, he is my kind of conservative:

> On the Normandy beaches Jeter would have been figuring out how to get up those cliffs at Pointe du Hoc. A-Rod might have been the best sniper, the most skillful rock climber, but he'd have been all too human, too anxious, too aware of his feelings, to take the kill shot. I recalled last night, those midsummer revelations of Rodriguez – that he had been in therapy with three different therapists at the same time: one for his marriage, one for his problems of early childhood, and one for his sports-related problems. Clearly he is immersed in our Oprahfied, therapeutic culture, where there's a therapist for every imaginable condition, as well as therapists ready to correct the actual conditions of life. He seemed determined to show that there really is crying in baseball.
>
> Could it be that the immense talent he possesses has been feminized so that in the showdown, the shoot-out at the OK Corral, where the masculine virtues – focused

aggression, the will to triumph and defeat the enemy – were absent? Is his talent undermined by softness of character and a yearning to be loved? How many times did he try desperately to hit a home run, only to wind up swinging and missing? What A-Rod needs is not therapeutic empathy, not encouragement to bare his soul and be more metrosexual. He needs to remember that baseball is a game whose object is to utterly defeat the opposition, preferably crush them so their defeat erodes their confidence. Self-reflection is not required and may be paralyzing. If A-Rod's reports of his fatherless childhood are meaningful enough to make him flinch from the ultimate triumph in order to protect his father from his own aggression, that is interesting to a psychoanalyst. But if it translates into a strikeout when he's expected to deliver a hit, such knowledge is worthless.

Hollywood: Where Everyone Learns the Terrible Lessons of the Blacklist (Selectively)

BUT FOR A FEW, PRINCIPLE MATTERS MORE IN LIFE THAN IN THE MOVIES

NOT LONG AGO, some very optimistic souls compiled a list of "Hollywood conservatives," defined as those with "the courage to speak out in an industry primarily flooded with liberals." You can find the list on the web under celiberal.com, and at first blush, it is indeed pretty damned encouraging. By my count, it numbers 321 names!

But don't look too closely. Listed are all sorts of people who aren't "Hollywood conservatives" at all. There are athletes (Arnold Palmer, Dale Earnhardt, Jr., Craig Biggio) and country western singers (Amy Grant, Charlie Daniels, Tim McGraw). There are "celebrities" you haven't heard from in such a long time (Connie Stevens, Doris Day, Art Linkletter) – you're not even sure they're still alive! – and then there are a whole bunch about as famous as your next door neighbor (Nappy Roots, Jeff "Skunk" Baxter, Wynn Varble). A few qualify less as famous than bizarre (Gary Coleman). And that's before you get to the ones you know perfectly well aren't conservative at all – in fact, in some cases, would rather face a career-threatening child pornography rap than have the damning adjective attached to their name. Jerry Seinfeld? Michael J. Fox? And by what lunatic definition does foul-mouthed, Bush-

Derangement-vet Kathy Griffin make such a list? Why not Alec Baldwin? Or Sharon Stone? Or *Oliver* Stone?

True, among all these, there are handful of actual Hollywood celebs with legit right-of-center credentials: Patricia Heaton, Dennis Miller, Gary Sinise, Ben Stein, Pat Sajak, Jon Voigt, Kelsey Grammer, James Woods, Bruce Willis, and a few others. In short, the Usual Suspects. Many are affiliated with a group called Friends of Abe – as in Lincoln – which reportedly holds social gatherings where members can commune without feeling despised. And, also true, Andrew Breitbart's terrific Big Hollywood website, covering Gomorrah from a right-of-center perspective, gives Hollywood conservatives a voice (even if sometimes anonymously).

So, yes, all this certainly gives hope to every starry-eyed conservative dreamer who for years has imagined ideological sanity and common sense (if not taste or standards) on the verge of a major comeback in the Land of Make Believe.

My friend Steve Finefrock, head of the Hollywood Conservative Forum, is one such dreamer. He maintains, straight-faced, that "conservatives comprise at least a quarter, maybe a third, of working creatives earning a paycheck in Hollywood TV and film productions," and that "a 'tipping point' is approaching."

Boy, oh boy, if only! But tell that to another friend of mine – let's call him Paolo Garboza. Let's call him that because he's threatened that if I use a pseudonym that comes within fifteen letters of his actual (Jewish) name, he'll sue me for all I'm worth – and that kind of threat, coming from a Hollywood type, is always to be taken seriously. Paolo is an agent, representing mainly writers, which is to say his livelihood depends on the goodwill of producers and studio executives. He's also a lifelong conservative, as passionate about his politics as anyone you'll ever meet. In private, that is.

I ask if he knows for a fact of anyone getting blackballed in Hollywood for having the wrong politics.

"For a fact? How do you prove a negative – that that's why someone *doesn't* get a job? But I'll tell you what I do know: This is a relationships business, people like to work with people they're comfortable with, not with people they hate." He stops, laughs. "I'm still 'Paolo,' right?"

What about him, I ask. Are any of the hard-core liberals with whom he does business aware of this double life of his?

"Are you kidding? During the Democratic primary fight, I had a Hillary placard on my front door and an Obama sign on my roof – facing the studios."

But aren't a number of industry conservatives perfectly open about their politics? What about those Friends of Abe? And the producer-director Jerry Zucker, a post-9/11 convert to the side of the angels, whose liberal-mocking *An American Carol* was a source of such hope to conservatives in the fall of 2008 before crashing at the box office?

"Listen, no matter what you hear, it's still a minute percentage of the industry – and even those people have to be wary."

And, true enough, as Stephen Hayes reported from the set of *An American Carol* in the *Weekly Standard*, when Zucker first met his prospective star, Kevin Farley, he "described his new film with words he had chosen carefully. 'I figured he was like everyone else in Hollywood – a Democrat,' Zucker recalls. 'And we knew that this was not a Democrat movie.' It would be a satirical look at the war on terror, he told Kevin Farley, and explained that he and [writer-producer Myrna] Sokoloff were political 'moderates.'" Farley, writes Hayes, likewise unaware of the filmmakers' politics, "answered with some strategic ambiguity of his own. 'I consider myself a centrist,' he said." In fact, it wasn't until he read the script that the actor realized they were all completely on the same page ideologically. "I thought that the minute we started talking about politics that would be the end," Farley conceded afterward. "There was this dance that we did – a dance familiar to conservative actors in Hollywood."

Indeed, reports Kelsey Grammer, who also appeared in the film, when he was still a relative unknown, he was threatened by a major sitcom director with the loss of a job unless he made a donation to Barabara Boxer's Senate campaign; he dutifully coughed up ten thousand dollars.

"Trust me," adds my friend Garboza, of Zucker, "almost everyone who comes out has already made it. Charlton Heston once said there are more closeted conservatives in Hollywood than closeted homosexuals. But that was around fifteen years ago. There are no closeted homosexuals anymore, and God only knows how many closeted conservatives!

"He also said he believed his politics cost even him some work.

"You want to talk Chuck Heston, here's the story that really nails it. When he was first diagnosed with Alzheimer's, George Clooney actually *joked* about it in public. And when it was pointed out this was in bad taste, Clooney said he didn't give a damn, because" – Paolo makes air quotes – "'as the head of the NRA, he deserves whatever he gets.' George Clooney, about the most beloved guy in this town, a fighter for all things good and noble!"

Of course, widely regarded as among Clooney's finest and noblest deeds was his work as director, co-writer, and co-star of the definitive anti-blacklist film, the Oscar-winning *Good Night and Good Luck*.

Ah, the blacklist! In Hollywood, the very word prompts wailing and gnashing of teeth. The ultimate in good versus evil, beleaguered open-minded civil libertarians pitted against the vicious and corrupt thugs of the right. Moreover, for many on Hollywood's deluded left, it is a scenario with enormous contemporary resonance, one that continues to play out in today's America. Forgotten – or, what am I thinking, never known – are the facts about that fondly remembered, martyred Hollywood Communist Party of the Thirties and Forties. It was totalitarian to the core, run by Moscow-controlled Stalinist true-believers; they had a dandy little blacklist of their own going, hired their own whenever possible, and denied work to political opponents. "The important thing is you should not argue with them," as so impartial an observer as

F. Scott Fitzgerald wrote of the Hollywood leftists of the Thirties. "Whatever you say they have ways of twisting it into shapes which put you in some lower category of mankind, 'Fascist,' 'Liberal,' 'Trotskyist,' and disparage you both intellectually and personally in the process."

"This whole outcry about betraying friends! Of course, no one ever does that in Hollywood," laughs another friend of mine, writer Burt Prelutsky. "The fact is, if everything had been exactly the same, except the names named were those of fascists instead of communists, they'd have been erecting statues to the 'informers' on Hollywood and Vine."

A onetime *Los Angeles Times* columnist who went on to a successful career writing for television (*M*A*S*H*, *Newhart*, *The Mary Tyler Moore Show*, *Family Ties*), Burt now makes his living as a conservative author and blogger, and is among the most astute – and fearless – observers of the Hollywood political scene.

Having grown up a conventional liberal, Prelutsky dates the beginnings of his rightward drift to his service in the late Eighties on the board of the Writer's Guild. In particular, he recalls a meeting where the board was considering a request that the union lend financial support to the photographer Robert Mapplethorpe, much admired by coastal elites for his "cutting-edge eroticism," who at the time was facing legal action for indecency. "So it's up for discussion, and of course I'm the only one arguing we shouldn't do it. I say, 'What kind of artistic vision is being expressed by aiming a camera at the genitals of young children? The guy's a pornographer!' Well, the vote comes, and I'm voted down 15 to 1. The attitude of my colleagues was on one side there's an artist and a gallery owner fighting for artistic freedom and against censorship, on the other side there's Jesse Helms. That's all it took."

He was so out of step with his left-liberal peers, and they with him, that eventually it became clear they simply weren't hearing the same music. "There was no anger. It was like I was crazy Uncle Sol who shows up at Thanksgiving and puts the mashed potatoes in his ears, and everyone says, 'Yeah, yeah, that's just him.' And I realized we'd reached the point where, as liberals, they felt truly they didn't have to listen or discuss. They're the good guys, and there *is* no other side."

Nowadays his active engagement with the enemy is largely confined to the occasional dinner party where, he says, when things get especially tense, his wife "sits there, very quiet, looking at the ceiling, pretending she's not with me." He pauses, then adds, "I do have an idea for a spec screenplay. It's set in 1950, about these all self-righteous lefties – and for once these schmucks aren't heroes and martyrs, but the ones who do rotten things when they have the power. Due to my lack of character, I finally sat down and wrote a first draft." He chuckles. "What's one more unsold spec screenplay?"

Knowing him, it's my guess that Prelutsky would be just as outspoken even if he were still dependent on the business for his livelihood, but he himself concedes that he can't be sure. "Let's just say my timing was good. It's a lot easier now that I'm over the hill. But I admire that brave and tiny band who do."

Yes, walking the dusty streets of Beverly Hills and Culver City, there are indeed some gutsy conservatives, relatively powerless in an industry that respects only power, yet unwilling to back down.

For instance, the director Chris Burgard. Invariably dressed in a cowboy hat and denim, he even looks the part. Burgard, a native of rural Wisconsin, arrived in Hollywood in the mid-Eighties as a dancer; his first job was as Matthew Broderick's dance double in the teen classic *Ferris Bueller's Day Off*. "But even when I was wearing tights for a living, I still owned guns and believed in God," he says. "My beliefs may be demonized out here, but they're pretty average in the rest of America."

Though he went on to appear as an actor and stuntman in numerous films, as well as on TV and in commercials, he early on determined he wanted to direct. His recent documentary, *Borders*, is his breakout film, guaranteeing his future.

Or, wait, correction: It almost surely would have been his break-out film – if only it were about something else. For while *Borders* is not overtly ideological, its subject is the mind-boggling chaos along America's southern borders, and it casts a sympathetic eye on the Minutemen. Never mind that it has been lavishly praised not just in the conservative press, but by the showbiz bible *Variety* ("a scathing expose") and even, incredibly, by *The New York Times* ("a terrifying glimpse of horrors too numerous to mention"), it runs seriously afoul of a community that prides itself on its un-wavering support (presumably excepting nannies and gardeners) of the "rights for undocumented workers," and so has been widely disdained, usually sight unseen.

Burgard and his wife, the film's executive producer, initially tried to get the film into the prestigious Sundance Festival. "I had previously been associated with two films that premiered there," he says, "so it seemed a plausible way to go. Well, instead of us, they chose a documentary called *Zoo*, about a guy who had sex with his horse and died of his internal injuries. I guess that's what they think America wants to see. It's pretty much a shorthand ver-sion of what my wife and I face in Hollywood."

For months they tried to land a distributor, before finally taking it out on the road on their own. It played numerous festivals, win-ning multiple awards, and in those venues where local theater owners booked it for their screens, it did good business. But, for-get Michael Moore or Al Gore, Burgard's film has never had a tiny fraction of the broad public exposure afforded even such second-tier, over-the-top liberal documentaries as Robert Greenwald's *Outfoxed* or Alex Gibney's *Enron: The Smartest Guys in the Room*. Even as I write this, I note that a documentary about the black-listed screenwriter Dalton Trumbo, described by the *New York Post*'s excellent critic Kyle Smith as painting "a golden nimbus of holiness" around Trumbo, is getting first-run treatment at two elite New York theaters.

"This is a town that usually goes crazy for whatever's fresh and new," observes Burgard. "Well, here's a low budget documentary that's sold over sixteen thousand units just through the website and filled theaters wherever it's played, and my phone doesn't ring. If this had been anything else, I'd have meetings at every studio in town and somebody'd be offering me money up front and a three-picture deal."

Then again, he went in with his eyes open. "People are more afraid to talk politics in this town than anywhere I've ever seen. You go on a set, and make some kind of politically incorrect comment, and it terrifies people, they're just scared to death they'll get fired. You want that phone to ring, you keep your mouth shut."

But that isn't Burgard's nature. He has a couple of other films in mind, and is upbeat about his prospects for lining up financing. "What I really want to do," he says, "my *mission* out here, is to make John Ford-type movies, movies that embrace the spirit of this country. Hollywood says you can't do that anymore. They say now you can't do a war movie, it won't be successful. That's just wrong. What people won't go see is a *defeatist* war movie."

Chris Brugard, meet Michael Mandaville, because if ever there were two guys who should be working together...

Mandaville is a veteran line producer and production manager, meaning he has day-to-day responsibility for almost every practical aspect of a film's production, from budget to managing the crew. His entry on IMDb, the Internet Movie Database, lists a couple of dozen films he's worked on, from *American History X* to a bunch of things you've probably never heard of.

Then there's his parallel life, as a fully engaged citizen. On his own time, Mandaville is completing an exhaustive, self published compendium of strategies for dealing with the terrorist threat entitled *Citizen-Soldier Handbook: 101 Ways for Americans to Fight Terrorism*. It is an astonishing research job, including everything from the particulars of intelligence gathering to combating media defeatism and innovative uses of technology. No fuller treatment of the subject exists anywhere.

"I see it as a starting point, something I hope will encourage others to generate ideas of their own," says Mandaville. "Because, no getting around it, this is a fight we *have* to win." And how does he expect this project to be greeted by colleagues in the business? "Well," he says, chuckling, "I guess I'll find out."

To date, he says, his politics have rarely intruded on his professional life. "I mean, I don't hide it, but I also don't make a point of it. I need the work. I need to feed my family." He pauses. "Actually, there's a lot more conservatism out here than you'd expect, just not necessarily where it's most visible. But I talk to people in construction, to teamsters, to people on set. It's true, a lot of them of them have trouble admitting it, the *word* fills them with enormous trepidation, but when you get on specific issues – the war, affirmative action – that's who they are. I tell them, hey, you wanna be hip in Hollywood, be a conservative. That's the real diversity."

Then again, as these things go, from time to time "something's come up" and he's had to take a stand, even if that meant "someone's cage got rattled." For instance, there was the film he was working on not long ago with an all-black cast and a black director. "So the DP decides there should be more blacks on the crew. He wants me to hire a black key grip and a gaffer. I told him, 'Forget that, that's not how I do things. I'm gonna hire the best people I can get for the price, regardless of color. I'm not gonna tell my kids not to racially discriminate and then do it myself. And, by the way, it's illegal and a violation of federal law to do so.'"

He pauses, thinking it over. "I guess there are times it's hurt me, here and there. But that's mainly with people I wouldn't want to work with, anyway. Sure, if I'd done things differently, I could probably be making bigger movies and more money. But you know what? At the end of my life, I honestly don't think that will be a regret. I really can't see myself saying 'Gee, if only I'd kept my mouth shut, I could've worked on *Spider-Man 7*.'"

I *Try – and Fail –* to Bridge the Gap

OVER THE YEARS, I've dabbled a bit myself in Hollywood – great money, lots of frustration – and back around 2002 I hit on what seemed a terrific idea. It was for a half-hour sitcom with an explicitly conservative point of view.

No, I wasn't kidding myself, or at least thought I wasn't. I was as keenly aware as the next conservative or libertarian that the business is overwhelmingly hostile to everything we think and believe, down to our preferences in cuisine (steak) and sex (heterosexual). But I also knew, or at least had certainly heard often enough, that Hollywood is a bottom-line town, with everyone, Obama-like, prepared to throw their grandmothers (so, presumably, also their politics) under the bus for a hit. Moreover, since it was soon after 9/11, at least some liberals seemed to have belatedly realized that a *lot* of Americans are conservative.

I called the show "Professor Paine," and in my proposal proclaimed that "it dares to speak the unspeakable as no character-driven sitcom has since "All in the Family." Each week it will zestfully skewer political correctness in all its many guises, and its protagonist, the guy in whom viewers will have a rooting interest, will be a character wholly unique in television – a likeable, smart, funny, and completely unapologetic *conservative*.

"The show will be set on a New England college campus where all manner of loony social and intellectual fads – from 'Take Back the Night' marches to attacks on 'dead white males' to lab rat defense rallies by animal rights activists – are in full flower; and yet where, for all the endless talk of celebrating 'diversity,' everyone is expected to pretty much think the same way."

The proposal went on to introduce the main characters, and describe a number of proposed episodes, some of them, in Hollywood-speak, "ripped from the headlines" – in this case, mainly from right-of-center publications and web sites few in Hollywood know exist. In one plot line, infuriated black activists on campus disrupt another campus group's picnic, making the idiotic claim that the term 'picnic' dates from slave days – as in 'pick a nigger.' (This actually happened at the State University of New York at Albany.) There was the one where radical feminists set up a "sex worker art exhibit" heavy on female nudity (happened at Bucknell), leading to a male student being brought up on sexism charges for "inappropriate staring." Then there was one – based, as we have seen, on painful real-life experience – where our protagonist's son gets in trouble with his high school English teacher for defending *Huckleberry Finn*, and our protagonist gets in trouble with his administration for making too big a public stink about it.

I'm not claiming that it was the funniest stuff in the world – rereading the pages now, there are definitely some things I'd do differently – but it was at least as funny as most of the stuff on the air, as well as a helluva lot more provocative.

Nor was I the only one who thought so. I got an executive from Viacom involved with the project, one of those rare, genuinely open-minded liberals, and he set up meetings at all the networks, plus the main cable stations. For a few days there, I thought it might actually happen.

Then, reality: I go into these meetings, one after another, and make my pitch. And every one goes the same way. It's not just that the executives present don't respond with hearty laughter; they express what seems like genuine bewilderment. Forget Greek – it was like I was talking ancient Minoan, and the topic was Hegelian dialectic. The premise is completely far-fetched, said their every word and gesture, and viewers will never buy it. What, exactly, was I trying to say, anyway? "You're not *against* feminism, are you?" one woman asked, with furrowed brow. (FYI, this was at Fox – no better than any of the rest.) Did I have a *problem* with diversity? Is *that* what the show is trying to say?

Let's put it this way: The week's highlight was a meeting at which some assistant served up an incredibly delicious raspberry soft drink that I haven't been able to find since.

Someday, perhaps even soon, there will be a breakthrough TV show, with values more common to Greenville, South Carolina, than to Gomorrah. But, trust me, it will take someone with a long resume, superhuman powers of persuasion, and, more than likely, certified victim status to get it done.

I Have Seen the Future
(*and It Stinks of Garlic*)

BEING A RED-STATE KIND OF
PERSON IN A BLEU-STATE
KIND OF WORLD

MY PREVIOUSLY-MENTIONED friend Denis Boyles is a terrific writer and thinker who happens to live with his family in France, beyond question the locale more envied and admired by left-of-center Americans than any other. Accordingly, I asked him to forward a sense of the place through his nearsighted but nonetheless penetrating Red-state eyes. His report:

> I first started coming to France in the Sixties, back when the whole country looked like a battleground, because, as a rule, that's what it had been for hundreds of years. I liked it; it felt like a truly foreign place with its rank cigarettes, its hole-in-the-floor unisex toilets, its hairy women, and its strange little phone tokens.
>
> Now that's all gone, but I'm still here, living on dollars worth a euro-dime, drinking cheap Vendean wine and trying to teach my children what it's like to be different from everyone around you – namely, a Red-state kind of person at leisure in a *bleu*-state kind of world.
>
> I still like France, but nowadays I like it for different reasons. Foremost among these is the ability to pick up a New York City newspaper, see a liberal politician advocating some goofy forward-looking policy, and say, "That'll

never work" – because I have not only seen the future, I'm living in it.

The new, blue world of tomorrow is here, in the heart of the Old World, in France. Every idea in Obama's left-wing playbook has been put into action here – massive tax increases disguised as "investments," comprehensive government health care schemes, massive educational bureaucracies, armies that can't shoot straight because they've forsworn violence, a fearful respect for religion so long as it's Islam, laws designed to keep politically supportive unions fat even at the expense of jobs, a knee-jerk hatred of free markets and especially post-Bush American conservatism. The kind of fantasies that Democrats in America go to bed dreaming about every night are all daily realities here in Europe.

So how's it going? Fine, as long as failure equals success. Let's look at these canards one by one. ("Canard" by the way is French for "duck!")

PUBLIC INVESTMENT HELPS EVERYONE. The "investments" made by the government of tomorrow require about 70 percent of everything you make, but in order to live in France with a carbon footprint the size of a stiletto heel, taxes will soon rise again, mostly on energy-related goods and services. Even the tax on gasoline has no apparent ceiling: The day a gallon of gas topped four dollars in the United States, those of us who live *bleu* were paying just over ten dollars for the metric equivalent. There's a tax on everything in France, including not just your income but the water you drink and, if you live outside an urban area, the fresh air you breathe. The VAT, a kind of mega-sales tax of 20 percent attached to every good and service and compounded with every transaction, insures a state of permanent price inflation (except where it inspires hatred of government and taxes – entire houses are built on the black, just to avoid the multiple taxes). This blue-state bromide will give you what France already has: many layers of government, reels of red tape, elevated levels of unemployment, and a nearly flat growth rate.

PEOPLE DESERVE TAXPAYER-FUNDED HEALTH CARE. Nobody deserves what Europe has. It's true that if you fall down almost anywhere in the EU, somebody eventually will pick you up. The problem is, they'll take you to a European hospital. You might as well fly to Detroit and throw yourself on the mercy of the ER at Metropolitan Hospital, since all the socialized plans in the EU are themselves on life-support. British patients facing death and waiting for the National Health Service to find a bed often ferry over to France, get treatment, then (if they survive) pray for reimbursement. The French system is bankrupt and unable to attend to sudden surges in patients. Proof of this came during a heat wave in August 2003, when 15,000 elderly French men and women died in stifling hospitals where there were no doctors and no nurses. French people who want dentistry done well and inexpensively book dental holidays in Budapest, where there's a glut of dentists, but a paucity of doctors. So Hungarians often shuffle off to Slovakia or elsewhere. And so on.

START SENDING KIDS TO SCHOOL AT AGE THREE AND THEY'LL GROW UP TALL AND SMART. For years, liberal Democrats have come to places like France, seen how massive an educational bureaucracy can grow if fertilized with enough money, thought, "I want one of those," then returned to the States to rattle on about "early childhood education," as Democratic Governor Brad Henry of Oklahoma recently did. To sell the idea of rapidly expanding the state's already expensive education system by including taxpayer-supported daycare, Henry told Oklahomans that the French system was "the best in the world." Except it's not. French drop-out rates are almost exactly the same as those in the States, and, as a French education ministry spokesman recently admitted, the system is "failing." It'll fail in the U.S., too, where there's never been proven a correlation between money and outcome. What it will succeed in doing is growing the state's bureaucratic groundcover and tossing lard at the NEA.

PENSIONS ARE AS SAFE AS THE GOVERNMENT'S WORD. The French "safety net" is like those in many European states: It's big, soft, and capable of catching middle-aged retirees as they fall off the payroll, then depositing them safely on a beach for the exceedingly long duration of their retirement. But the French emphasis is on adult gratification, part of a worldview (here, as in the States, pushed by feminism) that regards children as inconveniences to the career-minded. The result is the production of very few French workers. That means to support all those tumbling retirees, Europe needs lots of immigrants, most from the Middle East and North Africa. They come to France and build many, many minarets. And it's a good bet that having to pay for other people's retirements will become yet another thing for them to resent.

WAR! WHAT IS IT GOOD FOR? Absolutely nothing, which, if you're a European, is lucky, since you don't fight any. That's what America's for – to be violent and loathed for it. Until Americans stop waging war to protect them, the despising will never stop!

RELIGIOUS PEOPLE ARE DANGEROUS BIGOTS. "Christians" in France rarely do anything so offensive as actually go to church. Overt displays of faith are outlawed and since the state owns all religious buildings in France (law of lacite, 1905), many churches now basically function as nice places for traditional weddings and museums. The only overtly religious people in Europe tend to be Muslim. Are they dangerous? Ask Theo van Gogh. Dangerous – and fecund! Long suffering from a population decline, Europe is being repopulated by the overtly religious.

UNIONS HELP THE WORKING MAN. Especially if the "working man" is a bureaucrat. Unions led the fight against the evil bosses for a thirty-five-hour work week. The result is workers who work as little as possible, but still strike every chance they get. All in all, a clever device that keeps productivity low and unemployment in the private sector very high.

FREE-MARKETS ARE AN ANGLO-SAXON PERVERSION. If antacids cost in Bleuland what they cost in the USA, *pas de problème*. But they don't. They cost fifty cents each. Per *tablet*. That's a real headache, which is bad, too, since aspirin costs ten times as much in France as it does in the old U.S.A. It wasn't supposed to be this way in the EU, but it is – because if it weren't, it would be like it is in America, and that can only be bad. We all know Nicolas Sarkozy is pro-American, and infinitely better than what came before. Unfortunately, France still thinks a blue America is better than a red one. It's a kind of cultural colorblindness, I guess.

I should add that as a dreaded *néo-con*, I'm treated with a combination of condescension and pity, like a bewildered sap still lost in 1989, when the Wall fell. No one ever points out that Blue Europe remains entranced by the mores and values of 1968, the year Parisian students rose in revolt and threw some rocks at some cops. The veterans of '68 and their followers proudly call themselves *'huitards*. It sounds like *weetards*. If I were Barbara Walters, I'd call them that, too.

Making Book as
a Despised Minority

SURVIVAL THROUGH PERSEVERANCE,
LUCK, AND PUBLISHING BOOKS
MILLIONS OF AMERICANS
WANT TO READ

IN 1999, THE POWERFUL literary agent Morton Janklow sent
a book proposal by his client, former Vice President Dan Quayle,
to Ann Godoff, president and editor-in-chief of Random House.
The proposed book set forth Quayle's plan for restoring the pri-
macy of traditional values, and since Quayle's previous book, his
memoir *Standing Firm*, had been a bestseller, this one promised to
find a similarly broad audience. Still, Godoff quickly turned the
book down.

While such a thing might raise eyebrows in the regular commercial world, it was pretty much business as usual for publishing; the book was also rejected by every other mainstream house
to which it was submitted. (It ended up being published by Word,
a Christian publishing house,) In fact, the only unusual thing
about any of it was the rare candor of Godoff's rejection note to
agent Janklow. It read in full: "Mr. Quayle's arguments will set
his agenda squarely before the American people. The proposal is
well thought through. The trouble is, I just don't want to be a party
to the promulgation of ideas I disagree with so profoundly. In the
end, I think the best publishing is done without reservation."

Just as telling, when Godoff's note became public, she was
scarcely even embarrassed. "'Other publishers turned down the

book, but I was the only one dope enough to put it in writing,' Ms. Godoff said with a bit of a laugh," reported *The New York Times* – and one can easily imagine the good-natured ribbing she took for weeks afterward at dinner parties for her truth-telling.

It's not as though anyone could pretend it was a surprise. In its deep and often irrational hostility to conservative thought – not to mention to flesh-and-blood conservatives – publishing has long been right down there in the gutter with its only slightly higher falutin' brother profession, academia.

Of course, the Godoff–Quayle imbroglio was a while ago, a lot of ink under the bridge, and the publishing landscape is very different today. Big-name conservative authors show up on bestseller lists all the time. Post-9/11, several of the largest conglomerates – Random House, Viking-Penguin, and Simon & Schuster – even created imprints devoted almost exclusively to publishing right-of-center books. The casual observer might actually get the impression that today the playing field in mainstream publishing is smooth and level.

Right, like Manuel Noriega's face.

Make no mistake, the creation of conservative imprints at the traditional houses, a grudging nod to economic reality, was a welcome development; they are staffed by smart, dedicated people, and they have published some terrific stuff. But they are the ugly stepchildren at those places, tolerated for their contributions to the bottom line, but seriously unloved, so always vulnerable to the vagaries of economic fortune.

What's ultimately more important is that recent years have made it clear that the mainstream houses are no longer the only game in town – or, for conservative readers and writers, necessarily even the primary one. As in radio and television, openly conservative alternatives, not dependent on the goodwill of those who, not to put too fine a point on it, despise us, have demonstrated their strength and staying power. From the conservative powerhouse Regnery to smaller idea-driven outfits like Ivan R.

Dee, ISI, and, yes, Encounter, small houses guarantee that right-of-center voices will never again be muted in the ongoing national dialogue about the crucial moral and intellectual questions Mortimer Adler once termed "the great conversation." No one knows better than the handful of conservatives laboring in mainstream publishing about the hostility of that world to all they think and believe. "It was total culture shock," says Bernadette Malone, former senior editor at Sentinel Books, Penguin's conservative imprint, of being recruited by Penguin from the conservative, Washington, D.C.-based powerhouse Regnery. "Everybody reads *The New York Times* every day and takes it as orthodoxy – and signs books on that basis! It was evident very quickly how insular the whole system is. They could all name three, four, five chefs, but couldn't name a single clergyman. The whole place felt very left-wing, über-cosmopolitan, cynical. It was actually funny – at first."

Malone vividly recalls the morning after George Bush's reelection in November, 2004. "I'm sitting there in my office, and a young editorial assistant walks in. Without a word, she raises her eyes to the sky, turns up her palms and wrists" – Malone demonstrates, making like a martyred saint – "and starts weeping in front of my desk." She pauses. "All I can say is, 'I'm very sorry for your loss,' which is what you say at a funeral, right? I mean, I really made a point of not gloating that day. It would have been too dangerous."

In some ways, to be sure, the episode was atypical. Collegiality, or at least its appearance, is very much the rule in the woman-dominated (and reflexively feminist) publishing business. While Malone describes one "very jarring" episode – after she acquired a book by Tom DeLay, someone in-house sought anonymously to smear her in the press – mostly what she got from coworkers was bewilderment and alarm: "People coming into my office saying, 'Can you really be pro-life and be a woman?' or 'Do you really think that torture is okay?'" Then again, she adds, "when I see Ann in the bathroom, we're always very nice to one another." That would be onetime Quayle nemesis Godoff, who now runs The Penguin Press.

But like other conservatives in a field dominated by liberal groupthink, she is under no illusions. Almost every one to whom I spoke offered some version of the same sentiment: Their more mainstream colleagues are perfectly civil, even friendly, "to my face."

And, indeed, when I asked a liberal longtime editor I know with a mainstream house for a candid, shorthand version of the assumptions she and her colleagues make about conservatives, she didn't hesitate. "Racist, sexist, homophobic, anti-choice fascists," she offered, smiling but meaning it. "They hate everyone who's not a rich white guy. The kind of idiots who voted for Bush and McCain."

"The fact is, very few of them know actual living, breathing conservatives, which makes it terribly easy to reduce them to caricature," observes Adam Bellow, Harper-Collins' go-to conservative editor. "After Bush was elected in 2004, and they could no longer claim he'd been 'selected,' it became an anthropological question for them: Who *are* these people? There followed a whole cottage industry of books and articles trying to prove that conservatives are a product of bad parenting, psychological syndromes, or genetic defects, as well as being generally stupid and evil."

This is what conservatives in the mainstream book business face on a daily basis: an even more self-certain brand of the familiar liberal mix of ignorance and contempt. Most of those in publishing know conservatives the same way they do terrorists, by unsavory reputation, the primary difference being that, in their view, at least terrorists have their reasons. They reflexively dismiss conservative books as, to put it charitably, unserious, written by people presumed to be committed (and generally mean-spirited) ideologues.

"As conservatives, living in their world, by definition we're exposed to both sides and they're not," notes Malone. "We're totally fluent in their language, but they hardly know ours even exists. So they're just shocked that everyone doesn't see things as they do. They demand: 'How can you question global warming when everyone knows it's a terrible crisis?' 'How *can* you question that the war's a disaster?' What's even more remarkable is they don't think of themselves as liberals. They're all 'centrists.' But they don't understand where right and left really are. To them, someone who's a moderate Republican is considered an extreme conservative. And someone like me is considered a 'fascist.'"

"The ideological consensus in publishing is so powerful and so internalized that those who exercise it are not even aware of it," agrees the writer Phyllis Chesler, a pioneering feminist long cele- brated by right-thinkers on the left (two of her books received front page treatment from *The New York Times Book Review*) until she became a pariah by breaking ranks after 9/11 by supporting the invasion of Afghanistan. "It's like a call-and-shout at an African- American church – if someone says 'Down with Bush,' the expected response is '*Hallelujah, down with Bush!*,' and if you don't make it, you're not part of the group."

Such lazy uniformity of thought prevails everywhere in main- stream houses, invariably shared not just by editors but by pro- motional types and sales people. "You have to reeducate them," says Adam Bellow of these last, "prepare them for what's going to happen when you publish a conservative book: You're going to get the bad review in *PW*, followed by the indignant column by Paul Krugman – but you have to let them know that, in this case, bad is good. We need our enemies, we cherish them. We use *The New York Times* to energize conservative media. I send every book I publish to Frank Rich, with a nice note saying, 'I hope you hate this one.' Unfortunately, they've gotten a little more savvy about being used that way, and tend not to respond. That's why I miss Anthony Lewis – he could never restrain himself."

What is even now only dimly understood among mainstream publishing types, if at all, is that millions of Americans are sick to death of a media, book publishers included, that treats them and their values with barely concealed contempt, and that these constitute a vast, *permanent* market for books. As Bernard Goldberg says of his 2001 blockbuster *Bias*, published by Regnery, "All I did was catch up with the American people."

In fact, *Bias* – originally titled *Media Culpa* – ended up with the conservative house only after it was turned down by every mainstream publisher Goldberg's agent sent it to. "He would call me," recalls Goldberg, "and report, 'So-and-so passed,' then read me the note from the editor. It would say things like 'This is well-written, but the premise doesn't make any sense. *Liberal bias? What's that supposed to mean?*' You know the movie *Sleepless in Seattle*? These people are *Clueless in Manhattan.*'"

Still, when the agent reported Al Regnery was interested in talking, Goldberg was initially unsure. "A conservative publisher? I felt a little funny about that." Friends told him going with Regnery would stigmatize the book, brand it as slanted by definition.

Thinking back, he's delighted he didn't listen, and, even more so, that the mainstream houses had no interest. "This idea that a Regnery book is somehow illegitimate is just incredible B.S.! Why is it that we're supposed to be concerned about Regnery being a conservative house, but nobody worries about all the publishers in Manhattan being liberal houses? It scares me even thinking about what would've happened if I'd gone with one of those houses. The book would've come and gone in a minute and sold exactly no copies!"

But Regnery knows its market and how to reach it in a big way. "Oprah is not one of the places we go for our books," says Sandy Schultz, who then worked with Regnery and now does publicity for a range of conservative imprints, "and we're much more interested in 'Fox and Friends' than the traditional network morning shows. The fact is, liberal producers don't want to give conservatives a platform. When Tom Friedman or even Al Franken has a new book, you'll never see someone on from the other side challenging them, but if they have on a conservative, they'll set up a debate format. The School of Regnery says, 'No media for media's sake, media to sell books.'" And, indeed, every publisher of conservative books today relies on the strategies pioneered by the Regnery selling machine, forgoing traditional media and aiming directly for the conservative base.

Bias, a book that might have disappeared without a trace, instead energized the crucial public debate on the issue that's been raging ever since. Conservative titles have similarly countered the left-liberal take on immigration (*The Immigration Solution*, *The New Case Against Immigration*); race (Ward Connerly's *Creating Equal*, Thomas Sowell's *Black Rednecks and White Liberals*); global warming (*Climate Confusion*, *The Politically Incorrect Guide to Global Warming and Environmentalism*), and the War on Terror and Iraq (*Willful Blindness*, *Moment of Truth*).

Alas, for some authors, having grown up hearing names like Knopf and Penguin spoken of with reverence, the realization can come too late that having a liberal-damning book published by a mainstream liberal house is the opposite of a blessing.

"Look what happened to that great book on the Duke lacrosse rape case," notes Goldberg. "If that had been with a conservative house, no question, it would've been a bestseller."

The reference is to *Until Proven Innocent*, Stuart Taylor and KC Johnson's unflinching look at Durham D.A. Michael Nifong's near legal-lynching of the three accused lacrosse players, and how it was abetted by the university's administration and faculty and the liberal media mob, led by *The New York Times*. Published by the Thomas Dunne imprint of St. Martin's Press, the book was much anticipated in conservative circles and appeared to great critical acclaim. Yet it died quickly, a victim of a publisher that utterly failed to grasp its potential appeal. "They printed only thirteen thousand copies and, as far as I know, gave it no advertising," says Taylor, who considers himself a liberal. "Amazon sold out the third day, and we got hundreds of emails from all over the country from people who couldn't find it in the stores, which killed it commercially. The truth is, the house just never seemed very excited about the book."

Taylor is a skilled reporter, and it did not take much exposure to those in publishing for him to figure out why. "People in-house just didn't seem to identify with the message of the book – and since they couldn't understand it, they had no sense of its appeal. That was also true of certain booksellers, who come out of the same culture as publishers and *New York Times* reporters. One woman told us she walked into a Borders and asked for the book, and was told, 'That's not the kind of book we would stock' – this whole idea that, 'Oh, this book is trashing the liberal media and left-wing faculty, so the hell with it.'"

Arthur C. Brooks, author of *Who Really Cares*, about charitable giving in America, had a similar experience. At the time a professor at Syracuse University and now president of the American Enterprise Institute, his research had led him to the highly illuminating conclusion that in fact conservatives give a good deal more than liberals. Clearly this was a book that conservatives, accustomed to being smeared as heartless and nasty, were likely to respond to in a big way. Yet, notes Brooks, when he was putting together the proposal, "a couple of people who are very close to me very strongly counseled against going to Regnery or any other conservative house. They said it would brand the book as right-wing and destroy its credibility. Better even to go to an academic press."

He ended up with Basic Books, a small mainstream house with an academic bent. The book was launched in late 2006 with no expectations and a print run of ten thousand copies – making for an average of two copies in each Barnes and Noble store – but with a surge of support from conservative media, including prized appearances on Rush Limbaugh and Bill O'Reilly's shows, it took off. The print run was so small, however, that it sold out two weeks before Christmas. More disappointing to Brooks was that the book achieved virtually no notice beyond conservative precincts. Indeed, it was almost impossible to find a liberal who even knew it existed, since it went unreviewed and unremarked upon by *The New York Times* and the *Washington Post* and was never covered on any network news program or NPR. "It was really striking," says Brooks. "If we could have had a generalized debate in the culture – if CNN had been willing to cover the subject the way Fox did – the impact could have been so much greater. Fox was all over this like a cheap suit. But Fox is behind a firewall."

Adam Bellow, who edited Jonah Goldberg's bestseller *Liberal Fascism* at Doubleday, notes that the company initially printed a mere fourteen thousand copies, and "just eked the book out into the marketplace, reprinting in quantities of five or ten thousand. If this had been a book by a major liberal journalist, they would have gone out with thirty thousand copies and reprinted in increments of twenty, and we would have been up to 150,000 in no time, with huge stacks in Barnes and Noble. Even when Jonah's book hit number one, it still wasn't easily obtainable. You'd walk into a Barnes and Noble and, if they had it at all, it would be tucked away on the second floor in the back in the 'Sociology' section."

To be sure, the mainstream conservative imprints have produced their fair number of big sellers, and also done their bit for conservative intellectual life. Crown Forum has published not only Ann Coulter, but also George Will, Ronald Kessler, and M. Stanton Evans, as well as provocative titles like *Who Killed the Constitution?* and Dan Flynn's *A Conservative History of the American Left*. Simon and Schuster's Threshold Editions, which got off to a slow start, produced John Bolton's *Surrender Is Not an Option* and Al Regnery's *Upstream: The Ascendancy of American Conservatism*. Penguin's Sentinel has to its credit Nonie Darwish's *Now They Call Me Infidel*, Mona Charen's *Do Gooders*, and Nicholas Wapshott's *Reagan and Thatcher*.

"Actually, Crown Forum publishes a lot of books that, if liberals read them, they'd benefit, because they'd be forced to grapple with new ideas," says the gentlemanly Jed Donahue, until recently the imprint's senior editor, specifically citing Byron York's critique of liberalism, *The Vast Left-Wing Conspiracy*. "But of course they'd never touch a book like that with a ten-foot pole."

Of course, that is the question mark hanging over the future of all the conservative imprints: Overwhelmingly, those who'll decide their fate regard them with what might be called a marked deficit of goodwill. Where comparable liberal imprints may get cut a break or three, the conservative imprints must succeed, over and over, or perish. While those who run them have performed good and noble service, working, as it were, within the system, the question, as always, is whether the system gives a damn about them.

"My own feeling is that these imprints are *designed* to fail," says Adam Bellow. "Management would be happy to see them succeed for financial reasons – yet because they basically see this type of publishing as deeply distasteful, an alien organism within the publishing body – they'd be just as happy if they fail. Then they could say, 'See, we tried, this kind of publishing is not a good business' and move on."

"When it comes to conservative books, the large publishing houses have always held their noses," agrees Regnery publisher Marji Ross. "My guess is that if they survive at all, they'll transition from conservative politics to just politics and current events. That's always been our advantage at Regnery. We are what we are; we're not going to morph into anything else."

Then again, the question itself is increasingly irrelevant. For the meaning of the past decade is that, one way or another, conservative publishing will survive – and thrive – on its own terms.

Of course, liberals will be the last to grasp that their power as arbiters of intellectual respectability has evaporated to near nothingness. They still have their prizes and honors, and don't hold your breath waiting for even the most gifted conservative writer – think Mark Steyn – to pick up a Pulitzer or a National Book Award.

But this is yet another arena where the words that bother them more than any others are right on target: Who cares?

Our Guaranteed
First Amendment Right
to Tell 'Em to Shove It!

ON JUNE 28, 2008, the publisher of this book, Roger Kimball, issued a statement that attracted considerable attention in publishing circles. He announced that, in light of *The New York Times*'s history of ignoring or, when it deigns to notice, trashing even the most important conservative titles, Encounter would no longer send its books to the paper for review. "Once upon a time," he wrote, "and not that long ago, it meant something if your book was reviewed in *The New York Times Book Review*. A *Times* review imparted a vital existential certification as well as a commercial boost. Is that still the case? Less and less, I believe. The *Times* in general has lost influence as the paper has receded into parochial, left-liberal boosterism and politically correct reportage."

It must be said that there were a few conservative observers of the New York literary scene who viewed this with mixed feelings. While one anonymous commentator on the web spoke for most in exulting, "Thank you Roger Kimball for being one of the few conservatives with the stones to tell the *Times* to shove it," many fretted that the *Times* still exercises great power, so ought not be needlessly crossed.

Me, I was with the guy who wrote: "This is wonderful news. *The New York Times* deserves to be marginalized. We must strive towards the day when people can care less about its very existence. Censorship is not the answer. We merely need to exercise our First Amendment-guaranteed right to neither purchase a copy of the *Times* – nor go out of our way to read it."

Indeed, my only quibble with Kimball's broadside was his assertion that "a positive review in the *Times* still helps sell books." Having been on both ends of that proposition, giving and receiving, I very seriously doubt that, at least when it comes to conservative titles. My *Right-Wing Conspiracy* book got an excellent review (albeit one of those very brief ones) in the *Book Review*, and I doubt it sold a single copy. Some years later, I gave an equally positive review in the same publication to Michael Medved's memoir *Right Turns*, with what was surely the same non-result. Except for the editor assigned to deal with me at the *Book Review*, who made no effort to hide his distaste for the review, no one I knew so much as mentioned having read it.

Why does any of this matter? In many, many parts of this glorious land, it doesn't. But conservatives in deep blue locales must live with the reality that, for their friends and neighbors, the *Times* is sacred text, the definitive guide for left-of-center Dittoheads on what matters and how to think about it, an emblem of superior intellect and morality. For these, as the paper's ubiquitous TV subscription ad has it: "There's the *Times* and there's everything else."

The difference between us and them is we understand that this is not only patently absurd, but that believing it, as Dr. Rossiter points out, is very likely a form of mental illness. There's a parody of the *Times* ad on YouTube that gets it just about right. "I love being the smartest person I know," intones one young woman, zombie-like, looking up from the paper. "*The New York Times* tells me about little brown people from across the world and what they're doing, because I need to know," agrees a smilingly blank young man.

As the drive by media's number-one hit squad, the *Times* does its dirty work on a daily basis, (with extra large doses of malice on Sunday). True enough, occasionally the paper will surprise. On Independence Day weekend, its Sunday *Magazine* ran a profile of Rush Limbaugh that was actually a fair, even sympathetic, look at the talented and complex man whose influence on our time has been significant almost beyond measure. Reading it, I kept thinking of the consternation and deep confusion it was surely arousing in *Times* readers, long having been instructed that Rush was the reactionary devil incarnate, and his millions of devoted listeners brain-dead yokel automatons. In fact, in its single most delightful passage, the piece points to Pew Research showing that on "news knowledge questions," Limbaugh listeners score higher than those devoted to NPR.

The *Times* does this from time to time, not merely tossing a bone to its critics on the Right, but one so large as to give pause, and maybe even hope, to the steeliest realists in conservative ranks. Who can forget the late and much lamented Michael Kelly's 1993 *Times Magazine* piece, "Saint Hillary" (complete with a cover illustration of the First Lady as a martyr), exposing the previously untouchable Hillary as the preening, platitude-spouting, moralizing gasbag she was?

The thinking here is evident. *Slanted? Us? Didn't you read our piece on Limbaugh? Or the latest David Brooks column? Or our public editor's mildly taking us to task for that vicious, evidence-light hit piece insinuating John McCain had a dalliance with a comely young lobbyist?*

But wise conservatives know better: It's not like anything ever seriously changes. To be suckered by this or that exception to the rule is, inevitably, to be doubly disheartened the same day by several things elsewhere in the paper, and the day after, and the day after that. Maybe it's another glowing review in the arts section of another perversity-fest. Or another lecture on diversity in the sports pages. Or another piece on food or fashion that out of the blue sticks in a gratuitous attack on conservatives, or Republicans, or the War on Terror. The magazine? My wife was still steaming about a cover story a couple of weeks before – on Father's Day! – once again slamming men for failing to live up to the *Times*'s standard of child-sharing equality, and crediting (guess who?) lesbian couples with being the best role models in that department.

For many of us, this leads to the question, and the philosophical challenge, of what to do about it. Must we continue daily suffering the slings and arrows of outrageous left-of-center nonsense even in the privacy of our homes? Living as we do in the midst of those fundamentally different from ourselves, must we also be *of* them? Do we not owe it to ourselves and our posterity to declare our independence and cancel the damn rag?

In recent years, countless blue state conservatives have answered with a resounding "Yes!" and at last, a few years ago, worn down, my wife and I were ready to join them. She had just one caveat. She loved the crossword puzzle, especially on weekends, and wasn't ready to give up that. Fine, I said, I'd get Xerox copies of the Saturday and Sunday puzzle. No, she said, that wasn't good enough, she liked doing it in the actual paper. Fine, I'd try and fish it out of our neighbors' recycling. Uh uh, then it would be old.

A difficult woman, but a principled one, and at last she agreed to make the requisite sacrifice. The paper has ceased to darken our doorstep and our breakfast table is immeasurably happier for it.

The *Times*'s subscription department, evidently still unaccustomed to such effrontery, seemed incredulous. Almost immediately the solicitations started arriving, seeking to woo us back with better and better deals, until they were pretty much giving the thing away. On receipt of the first such offer, I wrote back explaining exactly why we'd dropped the paper, as I'd earlier expressed my dissatisfaction to the woman on the phone when we cancelled. When the solicitations kept coming, I at length wrote back again.

To Whom It May Concern:

Thank you for continuing to pursue us as *New York Times* subscribers. In light of the difficult economic times, as well as the obvious deterioration in the quality of the newspaper, in lieu of your proposed rate, herein a counter-offer: Seven days a week home delivery of the *Times* at the rate of one dollar ($1.00) per week.

Trusting you will find this acceptable, please find enclosed a check for twenty-six dollars ($26.00) to cover a six-month subscription.

Sincerely,

For now, that seems to have done the trick.

It's not that I never see the *Times* at all anymore. When someone I respect mentions an article that sounds interesting, I might Nexis it – that's how I got the Limbaugh piece – and when I go to the city by train, I'll often find a copy in a Grand Central trash bin (even if this sometimes involves tearing off a corner bearing a fresh coffee stain or a piece of gum). Reading the thing, I can be reminded that plenty of interesting stuff runs in, say, the science section, but almost always, too, I run across some nausea-inducing something (in addition to the coffee and the gum) that makes me glad anew that we now subsidize the *Wall Street Journal* and the *New York Post* instead.

"If I am not for myself, who is for me?" observed the Hebrew sage Hillel, who, I like to think, would've cancelled his *Times* subscription based on the paper's Israel coverage alone.

If we had even fleeting doubts about our decision to banish the offending rag from our domain, they were utterly put to rest by the *Times*'s performance during the 2008 presidential campaign. "Cheerleading" doesn't begin to tell it – we're talking a dogged, scorched-earth campaign on behalf of the Chosen One, everything from burying potentially damaging stories to reflexively smearing as racist those seeking to give those stories the play they deserved.

In this, the *Times* gave cover for liberals everywhere in Obamaland, who, feeling themselves on the precipice of history, were even more fervent in their moral self regard than usual, so even less willing to credit Obama's opponents with basic decency. By almost every account, leftist vandals went crazy in 2008, with more Republican cars keyed and yard signs defaced than ever before. But even more telling was the venom that came so readily to the lips of ordinary, run-of-the-mill non-thug libs. A much-viewed video on YouTube, showed an intrepid band of McCain supporters who dared to parade through a street fair on New York's Upper West Side. At every turn met with the kind of brute, face-twisting hatred that once greeted civil rights marchers in the South. "Something's happening here, and it's getting scary," wrote conservative Portland *Oregonian* columnist David Rheinhard, of an intolerance afoot in that deep blue corner of the world that, for him, had finally reached toxic levels. "I love politics and public policy, but the ugliness, the anger, the coarseness and even the threats of violence I've experienced as a conservative opinion-writer in achingly 'tolerant' Portland have contributed to my decision to leave the business after this election. My heart was starting to harden – do we conservatives not have hearts, do we not bleed? – and I didn't want that to happen . . . the constant expletive-laced rants, the nifty Nazi–Hitler–German references, the holier-than-thou hate for any opposing view from the half-informed – well, it's not what our public discourse should be."

But maybe the most revealing episode involved a fourteen-year old girl named Catherine Vogt in the left-leaning Chicago suburb of Oak Park. As an experiment, she wore a pro-McCain shirt to her middle school one day, and a pro-Obama shirt the next. Even she seemed startled by how much grief she took as McCain Girl. Repeatedly, she was told "to go die. It was a lot of dying. A lot of comments about how I should be killed." Among the suggested methods: She should be "crucifixed" (*sic*) and "burned with her shirt on" for "being a filthy-rich Republican." Then she put on her Obama Girl shirt and, yea, it was as if the heavens had opened and she had seen the light. "They said things like my brain had come back. . ."

Of course, none of this will register as news to conservatives in deep blue America: in various ways, we get crucified all the time. Here in the New York suburbs, we have one brave Republican neighbor who, struck by the tenor of the campaign, was moved to write to the local paper that the "far left is tolerant as long as you agree with them. If not, watch out. You will be labeled as bigoted, homophobic, evil, scary, and, if those don't work, downright stupid." In the following week's letters section came the furious, all-too-predictable counter-attack, a barrage that began with – what else – a charge of McCarthyism: Critic of left-wing politics "embraces 1950's red-baiting" tactic, as the headline had it.

Indeed, it is striking how little grace many liberals showed even after the long- awaited triumph. A day or two of gloating was fine, even understandable, as was the sudden keen sense of disorientation on our side. But then we got over it. In the weeks following Barack Obama's election, I heard from at least a dozen conservatives some variation on the theme that Obama is all our president now, and for the country's sake, we must wish him well. In contrast, more than a few liberals I know remained as angry as ever, still cursing out Bush, Cheney, and their most recent object of scorn, Palin. Some of these people had defiantly left on their Kerry–Edwards stickers for four long years – and can there be any doubt that their Obama stickers will still be in place on that distant day their Priuses and Volvos get towed off to the great recycling heap in the sky?

"The frequently wronged, but never wrong, liberal American hard core," the *Wall Street Journal*'s Bret Stephens aptly terms them. Forever fueled by rage and a sense of ill-usage, in their view their problems, and liberalism's, are never of their own making but always the result of rotten luck or, more often, evil and corruption on the other side. Stephens's point is that now, with "a president who seemed to have stepped out of the last episodes of the

West Wing," who has "Congress in his left pocket [and] the news media in his right pocket (or is it the other way around?)," they will finally have to take responsibility if, and when, things go awry. The excuses will be harder to come by.

Is he thinking of the same liberals I am? Guaranteed, they'll have no trouble finding all the excuses they need – starting with George W. Bush and, for their purposes, the bottomless mess he left behind.

Of course, that's just another difference between us and them. Disappointed as we are by the results of the 2008 elections, steeling ourselves for the storm to follow, we conservatives face life as it is and press on, plucky as colonial Brits in those old movies on TCM.

Just a week past Election Day, Encounter Books threw itself a tenth anniversary party, a decade of steadily growing success, despite – maybe partly even because of – *The New York Times*. Fittingly, for an organization that prizes tradition and celebrates the glories of the nation's past, the event was held in the stately old mansion that houses the New-York Historical Society; and, just as fittingly, the atmosphere was the opposite of glum.

Conservatives mainly from New York and environs, these were survivors, fighters on a daily basis against liberalism and its manifold idiocies, and so not about to be discouraged by something so trivial as *The New York Times*'s idea of a revolution. There were many invigorating conversations that night, and much talk of revival. But the spirit was perhaps best summed up by my courtly, Louisiana-born friend Cortes DeRussy. He was among those who'd taken the McCain sticker off his car immediately after the election, someone for whom Country First, Party Second is not just a campaign slogan, but a life philosophy. "But I kept on the one for the New York Rifle & Pistol Association." He paused, smiling. "Just in case anyone thinks I've gone soft."

Index

A NOTE ON THE TYPE

"I CAN'T BELIEVE I'M SITTING NEXT TO A REPUBLICAN"
has been set in Sabon Next, a type with a distinguished and complex
history. Originally commissioned in the 1960s from the master tyopog-
rapher, designer, and calligrapher Jan Tschichold, Sabon is a contem-
porary interpretation of a roman type attributed to Claude Garamond
and an italic attributed to Robert Granjon. It was named in honor of
Jacques Sabon, a punchcutter who worked for the printer who created
the specimen on which Tschichold based his design. Because the types
were initially intended for machine composition on both Linotype and
Monotype as well as for cold-metal composition, the design was care-
fully drawn and modified to accommodate the limitations imposed by
the various methods of composition. This process resulted in a widely
popular type that was somewhat compromised by its lack of kerns, a
feature that limited the appeal of the italic in particular. Sabon Next
was drawn in 2002 by Jean François Porchez, who set out to harmonize
Tschichold's type and the types that inspired it with the possibilities
that the OpenType platform offered to the contemporary type designer.
The result is an elegant, highly readable type with a complete range of
characters (including a generous selection of ligatures, swash characters,
and ornaments) that is beautifully suited to book work.

DESIGN & COMPOSITION BY CARL W. SCARBROUGH